Bitcoin

A

Beginners Guide

to Bitcoin

By

James Tudor

Copyright ©2017

All rights reserved. Except as permitted under the U.S. Copyright Act of 1976, the scanning, uploading and distribution of this book via the Internet or via any other means without the express permission of the author is illegal and punishable by law. Please purchase only authorized electronic editions, and do not participate in or encourage electronic piracy of copyrighted material.

Disclaimer

This publication is designed to provide competent and reliable information regarding the subject matter covered. However, it is sold with the understanding that the author is not engaged in rendering investment or other professional advice. Laws and practices often vary from state to state and country to country and if investment or other expert assistance is required, the services of a professional should be sought. The author specifically disclaims any liability that is incurred from the use or application of the contents of this book.

Table of Contents

Introduction..6

Chapter 1 – The History of Bitcoin 9
- ❖ Chapter 1 Quiz 24

Chapter 2 – Bitcoin vs Traditional Currency 28
- ❖ Chapter 2 Quiz 37

Chapter 3 – Bitcoin, Cryptocurrency, and the Blockchain Technology 40
- ❖ Chapter 3 Quiz 62

Chapter 4 – Bitcoin Mining..66
- ❖ Chapter 4 Quiz 79

Chapter 5 – How Bitcoin Works 82
- ❖ Chapter 5 Quiz 102

Chapter 6 – Bitcoin's Record-Breaking Price 106
- ❖ Chapter 6 Quiz 120

Chapter 7 – Is Bitcoin the Right Investment for You?.................................123
- ❖ Chapter 7 Quiz 132

Chapter 8 – How to Make Money in Bitcoin 135
- ❖ Chapter 8 Quiz 154

Chapter 9 – Bitcoin Facts & Myths..159
- ❖ 20 Facts About Bitcoin 159
- ❖ 20 Myths About Bitcoin 167

Chapter 10 – Bitcoin FAQs 178

The End

Appendix A – Chapter 1 Quiz solution 189

Appendix B – Chapter 2 Quiz solution 191

Appendix C – Chapter 3 Quiz solution 193

Appendix D – Chapter 4 Quiz solution 194

Appendix E – Chapter 5 Quiz solution 195

Appendix F – Chapter 6 Quiz solution 196

Appendix G – Chapter 7 Quiz solution 197

Appendix H – Chapter 8 Quiz solution 198

Introduction

Thank you for taking the time to download this book: "Bitcoin: A Beginners Guide to Bitcoin".

Filled with current information and practical guidance, this book will show you:

- ❖ The rise of Bitcoin from a mere white paper to becoming the currency of the future
- ❖ How the blockchain protocol works and how people can mine for Bitcoins
- ❖ The advantages and disadvantages of using Bitcoins
- ❖ How to make money with Bitcoins
- ❖ Bitcoin Risks, How to Avoid Them and Manage Your Exposure etc.
- ❖ Bitcoin Facts, Myths and Frequently Asked Questions (FAQs)
- ❖ Quiz at the end of each chapter to help you consolidate your knowledge and understanding of Bitcoin.

Bitcoin has gained popularity in the recent years, and it is even pegged as the money of the future. Whether you are interested in Bitcoin mining, you just want a basic guide to arm you in Bitcoin trading or investing, or you are just plain curious about this cryptocurrency, this book can help you understand this emerging industry.

Once again, thanks for downloading this book. I hope you find it helpful!

History

How it All Began

Chapter 1

The History of Bitcoin

The money that we use every day has three fundamental traits: it is tangible, regulated by a central authority, and it can be faked. Bitcoin embodies none of these traits. It is digital, no one is regulating it, and it is impossible to counterfeit.

Although it is named Bitcoin, there are no actual coins that you can hold if you buy this digital currency. It is free-flowing because there is no one controlling and monitoring its footprints. In addition, it is not affected by the traditional currency factors such as deflation or inflation because market demand completely defines its value.

And finally, you can't reverse Bitcoin transactions. Once you initiate the process, you cannot retract it. The transactions can be done with total concealment of your identity, and the cost is very minimal compared to banks. Slowly, Bitcoin is now becoming as popular as other currency values. But, with no backing from the government, this cryptocurrency is only as relevant as deemed necessary by its users and receivers (consumers and merchants).

Historical Background of Bitcoin

In 2008, Satoshi Nakamoto published a white paper entitled "Bitcoin: A Peer-to-Peer Electronic Cash System," which describes how this cryptocurrency works. After only several months, the first version of Bitcoin was released. The first Bitcoin transaction was recorded between Satoshi Nakamoto and Hal Finney, a known personality in the world of cryptography. The exchange rate between USD and BTC in June 2009 was only 1 BTC = 0.0001 USD. The exchange rate was based on the cost of running a PC to generate Bitcoins.

Very few people were aware of the existence of Bitcoin, and most of them were coders, programmers, and cryptographers who were constantly discussing the promise of the currency of the future in online forums. Eventually, an exclusive forum was created, which has helped coders to easily coordinate with each other to take part in the development of the open-source code through Github.

The Bitcoin protocol was considered as a breakthrough innovation in the field of cryptography, even though it is founded on early innovations. The cypherpunks, a community of experts in cryptography, played a vital role in recognizing the ingenuity of Bitcoin and helped in its development.

By 2010, the ecosystem supporting Bitcoin was mostly used for recording transactions. This is the early phase of the Blockchain technology. Payment processors and wallet services were still non-existent, and there was also no actual user interface. This restricted transactions between people who were aware and had the technical skills to initiate codes for the blockchain. For instance, a programmer in Florida initiated the first commercial Bitcoin transaction by ordering a pizza worth 10,000 BTC.

But the prototype of a market ecosystem started to rise. By the early months of 2010, the first exchange became accessible for anyone who wanted to trade Bitcoins. An article describing Bitcoin was published on Slashdot, a popular technology website, which stirred the interest between early adopters. After this, Mt. Gox launched another platform for exchange, which became a major trading channel for Bitcoins for at least two years.

By 2011, Bitcoin started to become an emerging system for virtual payments, even though its usage is still restricted by the aspirations of early followers. The anonymity feature of the cryptocurrency made Bitcoin an enticing channel for digital black markets. It also gave rise to the Silk Road, which was an online store for illegal items (mainly prohibited drugs), which used Bitcoin as a method for payment. Unfortunately, the illicit online platform was among the early introductions of Bitcoin to the public, which has prompted the government to investigate the currency for its involvement in drugs and money laundering.

It also resulted in media coverage with Time, Bloomberg, and Forbes writing about the cryptocurrency. Politicians warned their constituents about Bitcoin, and it also became the subject of academic discourse. Some TV shows also aired episodes covering or mainly focusing about Bitcoin.

By this time, other commercial services also began to emerge. WikiLeaks began accepting donations in the form of Bitcoin. Bitpay, which allows merchants to accept

Bitcoin through a phone app, was also launched. More Bitcoin exchanges were open, which allow people to trade BTCs for other cryptocurrencies as well as fiat currencies.

The Bitcoin code also underwent a significant change. Satoshi Nakamoto primarily managed the codebase maintenance, but he has never appeared in public and never talked to anyone from the community, except through online forums. By April 2011, Nakamoto appointed Gavin Andreson to manage the project. Andreson immediately appointed four other cryptographers to help him in maintaining the codebase, and they also developed several structured ways to update the fundamental Bitcoin and Blockchain code. It was also in 2011 that Litecoin was introduced as the first alternative cryptocurrency.

During 2011, the financial markets were doing well, but people were not happy. In September, the Occupy Wall Street began and soon Occupy protests were demonstrated in major cities around the world. The world saw the possibility of living in a world where we don't need to depend on the banking system.

By the year's end, more and more people became ambivalent about using virtual currency. Bitcoin was seen by the public as the currency of the future, while the government perceived it as a tool for purchasing illegal items and for money laundering.

By 2012, Bitcoin was riding along the trend for being legitimate in most areas, which had conflicting impact. It became a valuable target for online thieves and hackers. One example is the hacking of Mt. Gox, which has led to the loss of thousands of BTCs.

Black markets using cryptocurrency for payment transactions still operate with an estimated $20 million worth of BTC revolved around Silk Road in 2012. Meanwhile, a popular gambling site, Satoshi Dice, flooded the whole platform with very minimal gambling bets, which ignited a forum on dealing with micro transactions.

In general, the cryptocurrency community was experiencing the effects of having no centralized regulatory body. There were also no allocated funds to help in the development of the core codes, and there are no dedicated places to resolve issues.

As a result, the Bitcoin Foundation was created, which mainly works to conduct education and outreach, represent the currency to the governments of the world, and to manage the fund to develop the technology. Later on, the Bitcoin-central.net, a popular Bitcoin exchange in Europe, was granted licenses similar to banks.

As it attracted the attention of more states, the legality of Bitcoin became a major concern. The public is using it like a fiat currency, trading it similar to a stock or bonds, and downloading it like a digital product. The Silk Road and online gambling was a major concern for governments, and some merchants stopped accepting Bitcoin because of legal issues.

Broadly, 2012 was around the time governments saw the potential of a bankless society. Mainstream media such as Forbes published several articles focusing on the use of Bitcoin for international remittances. WordPress began accepting Bitcoin, citing the limitations of conventional payment processors that hinder bloggers outside the US and UK to participate in the blogosphere.

2013 was a year of volatility for Bitcoin where two significant fluctuations in the Bitcoin price were experienced by consumers. The first fluctuation happened in early 2013, when the European Union and Cyprus entered into a bailout deal, which included a levy on bank accounts with huge deposits. This has ignited account holders in Cyprus to purchase large amounts of BTC. As a result, the price of Bitcoin doubled almost overnight, and the Cyprus experience became a precedent for using BTC as a means to conserve currency value.

Bitcoin managed to survive a huge crisis in terms of legitimacy in 2013 when Silk Road was shut down by the federal government and its founder arrested. All assets of Silk Road were seized, and it has resulted in a wider association of Bitcoin to the black market. This led to a fast dropping of price, but it immediately recovered.

In the global arena, governments started to become more serious about Bitcoin. However, not all responses were in favor of the cryptocurrency.

The United States government heavily regulated Mt. Gox as a financial transmitter firm, and moved some of its assets. It also established among the earliest regulations governing the usage of Bitcoin via a guidance report for people who are using, trading, and managing digital currencies. Specifically, the exchanges should comply with the policies of the state on money laundering. The US Senate also called a senate hearing to discuss Bitcoin, and to the surprise of many, Congress declared its position as being open to the long-term potential of Bitcoin.

Meanwhile, after its prior approval, China decided to ban all financial institutions and citizens from using Bitcoin.

The next wave of Bitcoin's volatility happened in November 2013. In only 30 days, the price of Bitcoin jumped from around $100 to more than $1300. This resulted in higher awareness for Bitcoin, and it once again enticed media outlets. In only a short span, Bitcoin moved from an effective virtual currency to a technological breakthrough. The price fell again in the later part of the year, but it never went below $200.

The rise of Bitcoin resulted in the emergence of alternative digital currencies, which are similar cryptocurrencies based on an improved or a separate underlying protocol. The first was Litecoin, which was introduced in 2011, but only after two years, hundreds of alternative coins were introduced in the public. Some are scams, while some became quite successful and are still being traded today, such as Litecoin, Manero, and Ether.

Mt. Gox finally shut down its operations in 2014, which had a large impact on the legitimacy of Bitcoin because the platform had been the most successful and the longest-running exchange for cryptocurrencies. It was the foundation of the community and the whole Bitcoin ecosystem. The shutdown was abrupt, and leaked records revealed that the platform lost around $40 million worth of BTCs. Critics of Bitcoin were quick to declare that Bitcoin was a sham, and it really influenced the ability of the virtual currency to safely operate without any regulation or oversight from a central authority.

As a response, the governments began to implement regulations. The tumultuous end of 2013 resulted in the sudden awareness of the people about the volatility of Bitcoin. China ordered their banks to close the accounts of Chinese digital currency exchanges, although the majority of them cited legal flaws to continue their operations. The IRS mandated that Bitcoin should be taxed like a property, and the state of New York launched its Bitlicense, which is a legal licensing structure for commercial firms who want to receive and accept digital currencies. This was massively criticized by the community because the character of Bitcoin as an unregulated currency was deemed fading.

Meanwhile, Bitcoin gradually seeped into the business world, and many huge retailers started to accept Bitcoin payments. This includes Microsoft, Dell, Newegg, Tiger Direct, and Overstock. PayPal's subsidiary also announced its ongoing integration of Bitcoin on its payment platform.

People also started to see Bitcoin as a digital currency by using the underlying technology for other areas. This resulted in a rise of applications using blockchain beyond the scope of digital currency. This was termed Bitcoin 2.0, in which people can use blockchain technology to keep all forms of data. This included Factom, which built a layer of data over blockchain to enable a secure, verifiable, and simple method of keeping records. Maidsafecoin was also another protocol added to permit distributed storage of files to be added on blockchain, while Ethereum was a platform used by software developers to run projects on a distributed channel.

This signified the emerging notion of what early adopters had envisioned—that the cryptocurrency will become the bedrock of the evolution of the World Wide Web. Today is similar to the 1990s, and in the next few years, the blockchain technology could disrupt everything. The seed was planted, but alongside it, the reality that it will take time.

In spite of these developments, the price of Bitcoin started a gradual decline in 2014, which even plummeted below $200 in early 2015 and was really idle for months. One major cause of the decline was the introduction of new virtual currencies. The market share of Bitcoin declined from 96% to 76% in December 2014. Another factor was the sobering realization that revolutionizing the financial markets will take some time. Despite its idealistic sense of being unregulated, Bitcoin is not above the law, and it can be very complicated to paddle through financial law. Yes, Bitcoin can be disruptive, but it could be a slow disruption.

However, the basic platform continued to operate. There were still attacks every now and then, which included a substantial loss of $5 million worth of BTCs from an important exchange in early 2015.

World governments continued to study the effects of this technology while also reiterating that Bitcoin is not above the law. Silk Road founder, Ross Ulbricht, was sentenced to life imprisonment without parole, and the CEO of Mt. Gox, Mark Karpele, was arrested by Japanese authorities.

The most important shifts were initiated by the banking industry. Many financial executives started talking about distributed ledgers and blockchains instead of the digital currency. Microsoft also introduced its blockchain services, which provided a platform for businesses to try blockchain and explore how they can use it for the various areas of their operations.

This in turn flamed the rising interest in Bitcoin among the general public as well as financial traders and investors. The price of Bitcoin started to increase again as people began realizing that Bitcoin and the blockchain technology has a promise.

The protocol of Bitcoin was built to process about seven BTC transactions for every second. The blockchain blocks were not big enough for storage. Bitcoin users realized that it was only a matter of months before the whole blockchain would reach its limit, and if nothing were done, it could affect the growth of the currency.

This resulted in a massive debate on whether to expand the size of the blocks to allow more transactions or to find a new position for the Bitcoin blockchain as a layer for settlement while permitting other services to initiate transactions. Without a governing authority, Bitcoin forums do not follow orders, have no public sanctions, and adhere to no democratic rules. The Bitcoin Foundation started hosting events, and online forums such as Bitcointalk and Reddit became public discussion boards.

The debate was fierce, and no agreement was reached. This was a major blow to the legitimacy of Bitcoin as a currency. People considered Bitcoin's inability to resolve a simple challenge of expanding its size, and wondered if it was capable of dealing with other problems. People also began talking about other alternative currencies that could be as viable as Bitcoin.

In 2016, the popularity of Bitcoin continued to increase with the network exceeding 1 exahash every second. Meanwhile, the Japanese Cabinet recognized cryptocurrencies such as Bitcoin as having the purpose and use of an actual money, and Bidorbuy — the biggest online marketplace in South Africa — started to accept Bitcoin payments for their customers.

In Argentina, Uber began accepting Bitcoin payments after the government banned credit card companies from transacting with the company. Another major cyberattack occurred in August 2016 when Bitfinex was hacked that resulted in a loss of $60 million worth of BTCs.

Bitcoin ATMs started to emerge around the world with around 800 ATMs worldwide. The Swiss Railway also updated its ticketing system so that riders can purchase tickets using Bitcoin.

By 2017, the number of merchants that are accepting Bitcoin continue to increase. NHK reported that they have recorded around 4.6 expansion rate among online merchants that are accepting Bitcoins. BitPay also announced that their transaction rate tripled, and cited usage of Bitcoin is increasing among B2B companies.

Bitcoin also gained more legitimacy among legacy financial companies and legislative bodies. For instance, Japan finally passed a law to enable Bitcoin as a legal method of payment, and Russia declared its interest to legalize usage of cryptocurrencies in the country. Skandiabanken, the largest online bank in Norway, already started the integration of Bitcoin accounts.

In the first and second quarter of 2017, the price of Bitcoin already exceeded the spot price for an ounce of gold, which was unprecedented. It also broke its all-time record by hitting $2,000 in May 2017. The number of projects in GitHub related to Bitcoin also reached 10,000, while the exchange trading volumes continue to rise.

In August 2017, the price of BTC reached $4,400, but at the time of writing, the current exchange rate of BTC to USD is $3,710.36.

The Mystery behind Satoshi Nakamoto

A person named Satoshi Nakamoto is credited as the inventor of Bitcoin, but no one has actually seen him. Hence, some people speculate that Satoshi Nakamoto is just a pseudonym used by a person or a group who authored the original white paper in 2008 and developed the first version of Bitcoin in 2009. Take note that the Bitcoin protocol requires people to use a birthday for registration, and it is known that Nakamoto signed up and used April 5 as his birthday.

Even though it can be enticing to go with the imagery of Nakamoto as a quixotic, lone genius who invented Bitcoin from nowhere, this type of innovation can never be created out of thin air. Most inventions, regardless of their "originality", were actually built on pre-existing research. In the case of Bitcoin, there were many precursors such as the Reusable Proof of Work by Hal Finney, Bit-Gold by Nick Szabo, B-Money by Wei Dai, and Hash Cash by Adam Back. These early virtual currencies were created as early as 1990s.

The anonymity behind Bitcoin can be driven by two main motivations. First is of course the privacy. As the cryptocurrency gradually increases its popularity, which now transcends many facets of our global society, its creator will of course become an instant celebrity and will be under the scrutiny of the government and the media.

Second is safety. Considering its first year alone, there were around 33,000 blocks mined, which was rewarded with 50 BTC for every block. The total payout that time was 1.6 Million BTC, which is now worth more than $900 million. Because very few people were aware of the existence of Bitcoin that time, many speculate that most of these blocks were mined by Nakamoto, and so he is now a multi-millionaire. If you are worth $900 million, you can become an easy target for criminals, specifically because

Bitcoins are more like cash and less like stocks, wherein the private keys required to authorize the transfer could be printed out then hidden somewhere.

Mainstream media speculated some people to be the actual Satoshi Nakamoto. Top suspects are Vili Lehdonvirta, a well-known economic sociologist, and Michael Clear, an Irish cryptographer. Other media outlets also suggested that Nakamoto could be a group composed of three people—Charles Bry, Vladimir Oksman, and Neal King—who applied for a patent about secure channels of communication prior to the registration of the domain bitcoin.org.

Other suspects include Shinichi Mochizuki (a popular mathematician in Japan), Jed McCaleb (co-founder of Mt.Gox), and Gavin Andresen (Lead Developer of Bitcoin). In 2013, Techcrunch released an interview with cryptography researcher Sky Grey who claimed that Nakamoto is actually Nick Szabo, the creator of Bit-Gold based on textual analysis of the white paper in 2008.

Meanwhile, in 2014, Newsweek published a cover article featuring a 64-year-old Japanese American engineer named Satoshi Nakamoto who is living in California.

There are many other suspects, and all of them deny being the inventor of Bitcoin. But regardless of the anonymity of its creator, one thing is clear: Bitcoin is now an important innovation, which could change our world in the years to come.

Chapter 1 Quiz

Please refer to Appendix A for the answers to this quiz

1. Who goes by the pseudonym Satoshi Nakamoto?

    A) Gavin Andreson

    B) Mark Karpele

    C) Hal Finney

    D) The exact identity of Nakamoto is unknown

2. What was Silk Road?

    A) A piece of code that revolutionized Blockchain technology

    B) An online marketplace created to purchase illegal goods

    C) The name for the original white paper published by Satoshi Nakamoto

    D) The first open exchange for bitcoin users

3. Bitcoin is:

    A) Anonymous

    B) Decentralized

    C) Impossible to counterfeit

    D) All of the above

4. The revolutionary technology which underlies Bitcoin is known as _____

    A) Blockchain

    B) Bitlink

    C) Pay storage

    D) Cryptocurrency

5. Why did Mt. Gox shut down?

    A) The government intervened, deeming the exchange illegal.

    B) The company no longer wished to service Bitcoin users.

    C) It was hacked, resulting in millions of lost Bitcoins.

    D) A more prestigious exchange opened, and all users flocked to it.

6. What was the first alternative cryptocurrency, or Altcoin?

    A) Litecoin

    B) Ethereum

    C) Dogecoin

    D) Manero

7. In 2012, how did the government generally perceive Bitcoin?

    A) As a physical currency with intrinsic value

    B) As a valid currency which should operate outside the bounds of the law

    C) As the newest form of legitimate payment which would one day replace traditional currency

    D) As a tool for purchasing illegal items and for money laundering

8. How did Microsoft contribute to the rise of Bitcoin?

    A) The company purchased a large amount of Bitcoin, a trend which investors followed.

    B) The company introduced blockchain services, which provided a platform for businesses to try blockchain.

    C) The company publicly endorsed Bitcoin in a press conference.

    D) The company began an extensive Bitcoin mining operation.

9. The first commercial Bitcoin transaction was for a pizza worth _____ BTC

A) 1

B) .0001

C) 10,000

D) 100

10. Bitcoin is immune to:

A) Inflation and Deflation

B) Hacking and theft

C) Price volatility

D) Disease

Bitcoin

Traditional Currencies & Cryptocurrencies

Chapter 2

Bitcoin vs Traditional Currency and Cryptocurrencies

Bitcoin is a breakthrough innovation, and it can actually replace our traditional currencies. But how is this digital currency so different from the money we use today? A $10 bill also has no other value other than what we agree as a society. And if the future society decides it wants to trust the Bitcoin system instead of the dollar model, then it can really become the currency of the future.

In essence, Bitcoin is quite different from the United States Dollars, for example, because it is not backed by the US state. This means that no institution has the power over this currency. The mere fact that the US government requires all payment to be in USD builds a direct demand for it. This demand cannot be easily replicated by cryptocurrencies.

But if we look back at our history, the involvement of a government in the monetary system goes deeper than merely demanding tax payments in its preferred currency. Understanding this history is beneficial for us to understand the possible restrictions of virtual currencies such as Bitcoin.

In general, governments have the inherent right to control our financial systems. It is important to take note that the state values the system of seigniorage for its revenue, so it is quite impossible to let this revenue source be replaced by a private money source like Bitcoin.

At present, cryptocurrencies are effectively not relevant if you compare it with the USD, which is a global payment system. However, those who are expecting the expansion of Bitcoin to a global scale are also considering the possibility that Bitcoin will not remain exclusively in the private domain. Once it becomes wide and large, this currency will definitely entice the government as signified by the declaration of the US Senate to be open for the long-term purpose of digital currencies.

Meanwhile, the concept of private currency as a solution to the inefficiencies of the barter system has minimal historical importance. For instance, although people usually believe that precious metals such as silver and gold were used gradually by the private sector as another medium for value exchange, in practice, people are not sure if the metallic component of currency coins are equal to its agreed value.

Coins were only widely accepted as a medium of exchange when governments had standardized its production. The Roman Empire, for example, practiced the currency system. After its downfall, however, people gradually returned to the barter system. Advocates of Bitcoin also believe that the verification and security problems in Bitcoin are less likely to impact a virtual currency. This area is yet to be seen in our future.

Bitcoin enthusiasts have also cited their commitment to limit the supply of digital coins, but currency experts are not completely relying on these claims. They oppose the interest of those who are regulating these currencies, so trusting them may not be the best thing to do.

What Makes Bitcoin Different

In spite of certain exceptions, there are several factors that make Bitcoin quite different compared to our current financial systems:

Factors that Differentiate Bitcoin

a) Decentralized

Fiat currencies such as USD, EUR, and JPY are under the regulation of a central government agency, usually through the central bank. Hence, their production can be regulated. The creation and transaction involving Bitcoins are regulated by a code, open source, and will largely depend on the P2P nature of the ecosystem. No central governing body can interfere in the Bitcoin processes.

b) Value

Take note that a currency is only accepted as a currency if it has an agreed value. Any currency such as the Japanese Yen represents value because the Japanese government, its people, and the international community agree that this currency has value. Bitcoin follows the same principle.

As you will later learn, Bitcoin is created through mining. The effort behind the activity provides the currency its value, while the changing demand and supply results in the fluctuation of value.

The concept of work providing value to a currency is known as POW or proof of work model. This is also known as proof of stake in other forms of virtual currencies. The Bitcoin ecosystem generates value if the transactions are recorded in the public ledger as producing a block also requires work.

c) Virtual

Traditional currency is signified by an actual object (bills, coins) to represent value. But Bitcoin is digital, and due to this you can keep the value using a digital wallet. Hence, there is no actual object that can represent Bitcoin.

d) Pseudonymity

Bitcoin owners keep their assets in a secured wallet. The confirmation of the account holder is kept in an encrypted place that they can control, but not associated to the person's identity. The connection between the Bitcoin and its owner is pseudonymous rather than anonymous as the ledgers can be accessed by anyone. Hence, these ledgers can be used to access data about people who are part of the Bitcoin ecosystem.

e) Cryptographic

Secure transaction is a main feature of Bitcoin. This feature is used to control the production of coins and to verify transactions.

f) Adaptive Scaling

Bitcoin is designed to allow one block of transaction to be mined in 10-minute intervals. The algorithm adapts after 2016 blocks, which is about 2 weeks, to make the mining more difficult or easier depending on the time that it took for the blocks to be mined. The mining is easy if it only takes 10 days to mine the blocks. Hence, the system will increase the difficulty.

You should not worry if at this point you are a bit confused about how Bitcoin works. It can be a challenge for beginners to understand these basic concepts of Bitcoin. Moreover, each chapter of this book will help you learn more about Bitcoins until you become more aware on how this cryptocurrency can become the currency of the future.

Comparing USD to Bitcoin can be Irrelevant

Two decades ago, when the World Wide Web was only beginning to gain ground, it was in a similar condition as Bitcoin today. The Internet was slowly replacing common methods of communication such as snail mail and typewriters at a gradual pace.

These were not immediately replaced, but their relevance is slowly fading. As we pass through the 21st century, mainstream media has joined the Internet Revolution, which has caused media outlets, especially newspapers, to change their landscape and scope. As the Web increased its scope and influence, it was not commonly compared to the relevance of Time Magazine or the New York Times.

In the 1990s, very few people were aware of or even using e-mail, but after only 20 years, millions of people around the world are now using it for personal and business use. In essence, Bitcoin is now following this lead by creating its own technology for blockchain over the Web's current virtual blockchain.

The increasing influence of Bitcoin on currency systems as well as worldwide commerce is set to be in comparison with the depth of the Web's natural ability to evolve the way we all communicate.

Despite being a breakthrough technology, Bitcoin is not reinventing the wheel so much as it is setting the accepted wheel in the Internet world in a thrilling new perspective. However, this may take several years, or even decade before we are able to see how cryptocurrencies can go. Nevertheless, it is moving onward and upward, and a lot of people are now starting to gain interest.

Meanwhile, Bitcoin scared a lot of authorities including governments and the banking industry. This scare was so great that the technology was banned in some areas. . As discussed in Chapter 1, the prohibition of Bitcoin in China caused a crash in the BTC marketplace. It has also gone through the mess at Mt. Gox where bots were allegedly pumping the BTC price, which created a market bubble.

Other crucial factors include the Silk Road shutdown, the licensing controversy in New York, and the IPO of Alibaba. Despite all of these, Bitcoin not only managed to survive these ordeals, but conversely thrived and caught the attention of the largest retailers and companies in the world such as Microsoft, Dish Network, Dell, PayPal, and many more.

To put it simply, snail mail and e-mail are both used as a means of communication. But this is where the comparison ends. Nowadays, probably because of uncertainty, the value of Bitcoin is often compared to the United States Dollar, which is the reserve currency of the world and the most established, most distributed, and most liquid currency today.

People compare Bitcoin to the USD, because they are both regarded as currencies. However, the value of Bitcoin is now beyond that. Currency is just one of the many uses of Bitcoin. Its price is increasing by at least 400% per year. It is possible to send 100 bits of data inside a Bitcoin. You can send a small percentage of a Bitcoin to someone for your business transactions. There is also a market cap in the production of Bitcoin. Bitcoin distribution is completely decentralized, and it is also not restricted by any geographical limitation.

On the other hand, the US Dollar is somewhat similar to the Presidents of the United States—almighty, but they had their time in the world where they once ruled. Now, they are only part of our history.

The value of USD is established at this point solely based on its liquidity and strength as world currency. However, many financial experts believe that it is set for a substantial crash. The Recession in 2009 was only the beginning. The status as a world currency usually lasts only at a maximum of 70 years, and the USD has held this status for more than seven decades now. The influence of the US military force around the world, with more than 100 military bases, is the primary factor that sustains the USD. However, this may not last for long.

An important step in the downfall of the USD as a world currency is the establishment of the BRICS Development Bank, which is composed of Brazil, Russia, India, China, and South Africa. This organization now controls 40% of the currency reserves and population of the world. It was also surprising that the United States was strangely silent when BRICS declared that they are now working with each other without using the USD. For many years, these countries have been working on bilateral trade agreements without using the world reserve currency.

These countries believe that the US dollar has lost its intrinsic value, and it is only a matter of time before it collapses. Meanwhile, the value of Bitcoin rises year after year. Famous financial experts such as Robert Kiyosaki, Ron Paul, Mike Malone, Jeff Berwick, and Peter Schiff believe that the world economy will collapse once the USD falls. Even the legendary George Soros, who made $1 Billion in forex trading, believes that Bitcoin is only a prelude to what will be the ultimate demise of the USD.

But does this mean we will stop using the dollar as our currency? That is unlikely to happen in the next two to three decades. But once it collapses, and falls to its intrinsic value, cryptocurrencies such as Bitcoin will experience an inverse relationship to the market. Its value will significantly rise against the USD as it continues to fade away. The only thing that will stop this from happening is if the Bitcoin ecosystem shuts down.

Hence, comparing the value of Bitcoin to the value of the US dollar is not considered relevant, because Bitcoin will not replace the USD as the reserve currency of the world. Take note that the value of the Internet is not measured in its capacity to replace a certain number of typewriters. It is irrelevant to measure Bitcoin in dollars because they are thriving in completely different platforms.

Chapter 2 Quiz

Please refer to Appendix B for the answers to this quiz

1. What is a factor that gives the USD its value?

    A) The fact that the US government requires all payment to be made in USD

    B) The material it is made from

    C) Its intrinsic worth

    D) None of the above

2. The concept of work providing value to a currency is known as _____

    A) The Blockchain Model

    B) The JP Morgan Model

    C) The Proof of Work (POW) Model

    D) The Cryptocurrency Model

3. A Bitcoin owner is not anonymous, but rather ____

    A) Known

    B) Pseudonymous

    C) Nonexistent

    D) A cryptographer

4. Bitcoin is following the trend of which of the following?

    A) The Media

    B) The Wheel

    C) The Banking Industry

    D) The Internet

5. Bitcoin was prohibited in which country?

   A) China

   B) The United States

   C) Russia

   D) Germany

6. What is BRICS Development Bank?

   A) An underground banking organization for illegal Bitcoin transactions

   B) A multi-country organization that controls 40% of the currency reserves

   C) A company which is attempting to regulate cryptocurrencies

   D) A place for Bitcoin users to deposit their private keys

7. True / False: We should compare the value of Bitcoin to the value of the US Dollar.

8. Approximately how long has the USD remained the dominant currency?

   A) 70 years

   B) 150 years

   C) 20 years

   D) USD has never been the dominating currency of the world

9. Bitcoin has proven its resilience because it managed to survive which ordeals?

   A) The Mt. Gox situation

   B) The New York licensing controversy

   C) IPO of Alibaba

   D) All of the above

Bitcoin

Cryptocurrency and Blockchain Technology

Chapter 3

Bitcoin, Cryptocurrency, and the Blockchain Technology

Cryptocurrency refers to a currency in digital or virtual form that uses cryptographic technology to add a layer of security for the transfer process and record keeping. Because of this feature, a digital currency can be difficult to fake.

Being organic is a significant trait of cryptocurrency, and it is also regarded as the best feature. Again, no single body governs cryptocurrency, so it cannot be manipulated by the government or the banking industry.

Bitcoin is one example of cryptocurrency which uses the blockchain technology.

What is Blockchain?

A blockchain is a decentralized and distributed digital ledger that is used to record transactions across many computers so that the record cannot be altered retroactively without the alteration of all subsequent blocks and the collusion of the network. More on this later.

By letting virtual information to be distributed but not replicated, blockchain technology has established a backbone on the evolution of the Internet. Originally created for the Bitcoin ecosystem, the technological world is now discovering other possible uses for the technology. In essence, blockchain can also create other forms of digital value.

Like the iPad that you might be using to read this eBook or the car that you are driving, there is no need to fully understand how the mechanism of blockchain operates in order to use it. But becoming aware of this technology will allow you to understand why this will become a significant part of our future.

Blockchain as a Distributed Ledger

Blockchain refers to the public, decentralized, and virtual record of all transactions of a cryptocurrency such as Bitcoin. The most recent transactions are recorded then added in chronological sequence. It also allows market players to monitor Bitcoin transactions without the need to access a central record. Every computer that is connected to the network will receive a copy of the blockchain that is automatically downloaded.

Imagine a ledger that is replicated several hundreds of times across a computer network. Then picture that this network is created for regular updates, and you now have the essential understanding of the blockchain technology.

The information that is recorded on a blockchain will exist as a public and regularly reconciled database. This is a method of utilizing the network, which has clear advantages. The blockchain ledger is not stored in one location, so the records are public and can be verified by anyone. No central format of this data exists for a thief to steal or a hacker to compromise. The data on the blockchain can be accessed by anyone via the Internet because it is hosted by millions of computers around the world at the same time.

If you are familiar with Google Docs, then it will be easy for you to understand this concept. The conventional method of sharing documents with collaboration is to send a document to another person, and ask them to do some revisions. The issue with this method is that you must wait until that person sends the revised copy again before you can access the changes.

This is the current method in our databases today. Two users cannot mess with the same document at the same time. This is how a majority of the banks now control, transfer, and maintain money balances. They momentarily lock the access while they are making a transfer, then wait for the other side to update the record, then will re-access the record once again for update. If you use Google Docs, both users can have access to the same document in real time. This is similar to a public ledger, but this is a shared record. The distributed part will come into play if sharing involves several people.

Like the Internet, blockchain has its own robustness. By keeping blocks of data which are identical across the network, the blockchain has no single failure point, and it cannot be regulated by a central authority.

Since the creation of Bitcoin in 2008, the blockchain technology has continued running without any major interference. Problems linked with Bitcoin are mainly due to mismanagement or cyber-attacks. To put it simply, these problems are caused by bad faith or human error and not by the underlying framework.

Basically, blockchain is a system that works to bring users into high-level accountability. This means that we will soon say goodbye to errors (both human and machine) as well as missed transactions. And most importantly, the most crucial area where Blockchain could help is to secure the veracity of a transaction through public record keeping, not only on the primary register but on a linked distributed system of registers, which are all linked via a validation system that is safe from interference.

Blockchain's Transparency

The blockchain network resides in a consensus world of collective wisdom which runs automatic checks and balances every 10 minutes. A self-checking ecosystem of virtual value, the network can reconcile each transaction that occurs in 10-minute intervals. Every group of these transactions is called a block. There are two significant properties that could result from this:

- ❖ It is not corruptible, because changing any data on the blockchain will require a large amount of computing power in order to override the whole network.

❖ Data transparency is embedded inside the network as a whole, and so in essence, it is accessible to the public.

This is theoretically possible, but in practical terms, it is not likely to happen. For instance, taking control of the system in order to catch Bitcoins will also have the same effect of damaging value.

Nodes - the Basic Unit of Blockchain

Blockchain is composed of nodes. A node is a computer that is linked to the blockchain network via a client, which performs the task of confirming and relaying the transactions within the ecosystem. Each node receives a copy of the blockchain that is automatically downloaded when it joins the whole network.

In combination, these create a strong second-level network, which is a completely different version for how the Internet could work. Each node serves as the administrator of the blockchain and voluntarily joins the network. Hence, the network is not centralized. But every node gets a reward for taking part in the system, which is a chance to win Bitcoins.

Most Bitcoin users describe nodes as the miners of Bitcoin, but this is actually not true in the strictest sense of the word. As a matter of fact, every node is joining a competition to win Bitcoins by solving mathematical problems. Bitcoin was the reason why blockchain exists as it was originally created. But today, it is now regarded as among the many possible uses of the technology.

There are about 600 to 700 cryptocurrencies created, and all of them have exchangeable tokens for value. In addition, a range of other possible adaptations of the original blockchain concept are now in development or already active.

Decentralized Network

The blockchain network is a decentralized system. Anything that could happen on it is a work of the whole network. Several crucial impacts could result from this. In creating a new method of verifying transactions, some areas of conventional commerce may soon fade away. For example, stock market trading might become simultaneous in the blockchain, or it may make other forms of data recording such as land registry to become completely accessible to the public. Decentralization has been existing for many decades now.

A worldwide network of computers is now using the blockchain technology to simultaneously manage the database, which takes note of the Bitcoin transactions. Therefore, Bitcoin is managed by the system itself and not any single administrative organization. Through decentralization, the network can operate on a P2P basis.

Who is using the blockchain technology?

hat there is no need to comprehensively understand blockchain for you to have it become beneficial for your life. At present, the financial world provides the most robust case for the technology. One example of this is global remittances. According to the World Bank, more than $500 Billion worth of transfers occurred around the world in 2015.

Currently, there is also a high demand for developers of the blockchain technology. It is now possible eliminate the need for a third party to process transactions.

The general public was able to take advantage of personal computers with the introduction of Graphical User Interface or GUI that was launched through desktop computing. Likewise, the most typical GUIs created for the blockchain are known as the wallet apps that people can use to purchase things using Bitcoin and other digital currencies

Online transactions are closely linked to the processes of verifying people's identity. And of course, these wallet apps will continue to evolve in the years to come to include other forms of managing our identities.

Cryptotechnology

By keeping data within the platform, blockchain is eliminating the risk, which comes with the data being stored in a central location. The whole platform has no central exposure points, which cyber thieves can easily attack. The World Wide Web has security problems withwhich we are all familiar. We usually depend on our password security to safeguard our assets and our identity online. On the other hand, the security layer of blockchain revolves around encryption.

This is all based on the concept of private and public keys. The public key refers to a randomly created number strings, which is actually the address of the user on the blockchain. The bitcoins sent across the whole network will be recorded and tagged to this address. On the other hand, the private key is similar to a password, which will provide you access to their Bitcoin or other virtual assets. As a result, the data you store in the blockchain cannot be corrupted. But while this is true, it is still crucial that you safeguard your digital assets by printing it out, which is regarded as a paper wallet.

New Functionality Layer

Through blockchain, the Internet gains a new functionality layer, which allow users to directly transact with each other. In 2016, Bitcoin transactions were worth around $200,000 daily. Through the extra layer of security added by the blockchain technology, emerging online businesses are on track to disrupt the conventional methods in the financial industry.

According to Goldman Sachs, the blockchain technology has the highest potential, specifically in improving the efficiency of settlements and clearing. This can also equate to a worldwide savings of up to $6 Billion every year.

Blockchain and the Evolution of the Internet

Aside from being a platform for cryptocurrency, blockchain can also provide web users with the capacity to build value and verify digital information. Emerging business applications for the blockchain technology includes the following:

a) The Sharing Industry

With new companies such as AirBnB and Uber becoming global success stories, the sharing industry is now proven as a business model. But at present, customers who like to avail of ride-sharing service have to depend on Uber as a third-party provider. But if payments can be enabled through P2P, the blockchain technology can open the door to direct transaction between the passenger and the driver, which will lead to a genuine sharing industry. One good example is the Open Bazaar, which employs blockchain to build a P2P online platform. Users can download the application on their devices, and they can easily transact with vendors without the need to pay for transaction charges. The protocol implements a no rules policy, which means that personal credibility will be even more significant for these transactions compared to what is currently happening in marketplaces such as eBay.

b) Smart Contracts

Public ledgers allow the coding of simple contracts that will execute if the pre-set conditions are already established. One example of this is the Ethereum network, which is an open-source blockchain, which was created especially for this purpose. Although it is still in its infancy, Ethereum has gained a lot of traction in the last few years, and cryptocurrency experts believe that it has the potential to leverage the power of blockchain on a genuine global-shaping scale.

At the present level of development of blockchain, smart contracts could be designed to perform basic functions. For example, you can pay one derivative if a financial instrument has already met a specific benchmark through the use of blockchain technology and Bitcoin that enables the automation of the payout.

c) Government Services

By improving the transparency and accessibility of information, blockchain technology can become a catalyst in the way government administers its basic services as well as the result on polls or elections. Smart contracts can also help to make the process faster and easier. One example is the application Boardroom, which allows organizational decisions to happen within the blockchain. This could disrupt how organizations govern and how they manage digital assets such as data and equities.

d) Record Keeping

A decentralized method of keeping records online will bring a lot of advantages. Disseminating data throughout the whole platform will safeguard files from getting lost or hacked. For example, the Inter-Planetary File System or IFPS makes it easy to build how a public web could function. Comparable to how bittorent moves data online, IPFS can eliminate the need for centralized client-server interactions such as the present form of the Internet. A new version of the World Wide Web that is composed of decentralized websites has the potential to expedite the file transfer and streaming. This improvement is not only efficient, but important in upgrading the Internet's presently overloaded systems for delivering content.

e) Intellectual Property Protection

As you might already know, there is no limit on how you can reproduce and distribute information in the Internet. This has provided many online users around the world a huge reserve of free content. But this is not good news for holders of copyright, because they can lose control over their intellectual property. Through smart contracts, copyright can be protected. It can also automate the sale of creative content via the Web, which eliminates the risk of replication and redistribution.

One good example of this is Mycelia, which employs the blockchain technology to build a P2P music distribution system. Established in the UK by the artist Imogen Heap, the platform allows artists to sell their songs directly to their fan base. It also allows artists to license samples to producers and manage royalties to musicians and songwriters. These functions work through the smart contracts. This use for the blockchain has a robust chance for success because blockchain can be used to release payments in a small percentage of Bitcoin, which are also known as micropayments.

f) Internet of Things (IoT)

IoT refers to the network-regulated administration of specific forms of electronic devices. One example is the regulation of air temperature within a database facility. Through smart contracts, it is possible to manage the automation of remote systems. This can be done through the integration of network facilities, sensors, and software as well as the exchange of data between systems and objects. The result could improve cost monitoring as well as efficiency of the system.

The most important players in telecommunications, tech, and manufacturing are all looking to dominate the IoT. This includes At&T, IBM, and Samsung. An organic extension of current systems regulated by these companies, IoT apps will be able to be applied in a wide range of purposes from massive management of automated systems, data analytics, and predictive maintenance of mechanized parts.

g) Management of Online Identity

We have a specific requirement for improved management of our online identity. The capacity to confirm your identity is the cornerstone technology of financial transactions that could occur online. However, the resolution for the risks involved in security that come with online portals are not completely perfect. Public ledgers can provide better ways for proving who you are, alongside the possibility of digitizing personal files. Securing personal identity is also crucial for internet communications in the sharing industry for example. Nevertheless, an outstanding reputation is the most crucial condition for conducting online transactions.

Establishing standards for digital identity can be a highly sophisticated protocol. Aside from the technical challenges, an encompassing web identity solution will require the cooperation between the government as well as private organizations. The problem can be exponentially challenging if we factor in the requirement to navigate the legal systems in various countries. At present, online stores depend on the SSL certificate to ensure that the transactions online are safe.

h) Information Management

Using social media platforms such as Facebook and Twitter is free, right? This is not completely true. In exchange for using these platforms, you are paying these companies with your personal information. But through blockchain, you can have the capacity to administer and sell the information that their web activities produce. And because this can be easily disseminated in micro currencies, Bitcoin will be used to facilitate this transaction.

For instance, Enigma—a project in MIT—has the capacity to understand that the privacy of the user is key in creating a marketplace for personal information. It uses cryptographic strategies to allow individual information sets to be divided between nodes, and also at the same time process massive calculations over the data group in general. Scalability can be achieved by fragmenting the information, unlike in blockchain technology where information could be replicated on each node.

i) Stock Trading

Stock trading can also take advantage of the blockchain technology through the improved efficiency of the shared platform. Once implemented, P2P trade confirmation could become more instant against the usual clearance time of three days. However, this could eliminate the need for custodians, auditors, and clearing houses.

Several commodities and stock exchanges are now using early forms of blockchain technology for the services they provide. This includes the Japan Exchange Group (JPX), Frankfurt Stock Exchange (Deutsche Borse), and the Australian Securities Exchange (ASX).

j) Crowdfunding

Crowdfunding projects such as Gofundme and Kickstarter are now implementing the comprehensive framework for the rising P2P economy. The popularity of these platforms signifies the increasing interest of people who want to have a direct involvement in the development of specific products. The blockchain technology is elevating this interest to the next level by building venture capital funds through crowdfunding.

For example, in 2016, the Decentralized Autonomous Organization (DAO) of Ethereum managed to raise as much as $200 million within 60 days. Crowdfunders bought DAO tokens, which allow them to choose the smart contract project they are interested in. However, the project was hacked and compromised because of poor due diligence. But nonetheless, the test suggests that the technology has the ability to drive new ways for people to cooperate.

The Difference between Database and Blockchain

The difference between a blockchain and a conventional database starts with the structure or how the technology is organized. The database that runs on the World Wide Web usually uses a client-server network structure.

A registered database user who has the right permissions will be able to change the entries that are stored on a central server. In changing the master copy, each time the client is accessing a database through a device such as a computer or a smartphone, they can work on an updated version of the database entry. Database control is still within the circle of administrators, which allows for access and authorizations to be confined by a central entity.

This is not the case with blockchain. For a blockchain database, every participant could maintain, update, and compute new items within. The nodes could work together to make certain that they are all coming from the same sources, which provide built-in security for the system.

The effect of this difference is that the blockchain is well-suited as a way of recording specific functions, while a central server is completely proper for other purposes.

Basically, blockchain permits various parties that don't necessarily trust each other to access the same information without the need for authority from a centralized administration. The transactions could be processed by the users that serve as a mechanism for consensus so that everyone could create the same sharing system of record all at the same time.

The main advantage of decentralized control is that it could eliminate the risks of centralized regulation. In a centralized database, anyone with enough level of access could easily corrupt or even wipe out the data. Hence, the system will highly rely on human administrators.

Many human administrators have earned enough trust that they can have full access to the database. This makes it easy for bank databases to record the money they have in their vaults. There is also a reasonable purpose for a centralized administration, and it is actually more ideal to use in special instances than blockchain technology.

However, this also means that those who need to run centralized administration have to spend substantial amounts of money to make sure that the databases will not be compromised. If the system fails, then the data could be leaked out or even stolen.

Many centralized databases are keeping information that is updated at a certain period of time. But more often than not, these are snapshot of a period that contains outdated information. On the other hand, blockchain systems are capable of keeping relevant information. Blockchain technology could create databases, which can create records of past transactions. They are capable of expanding its previous transactions into an archive while simultaneously offering real-timeimages.

While you can use blockchain systems to act as a records system as well as a platform for facilitating transactions, they are regarded as slow when you compare them to current technologies for digital transactions such as the technologies used by PayPal and Visa. Although it is also certain that the blockchain technology will be further improved in the future, the core structure of the blockchain technology calls for some speed to be left on the wayside.

The system of distributing the networks is used in blockchain so they compound and not share processing speed and power. They each separately provide service to the whole network, and then do some comparison checks with the whole network, until the whole system agrees that the transactions are genuine. On the other hand, centralized databases are used and have been improved significantly ever since their advent in many industries.

Take note that Bitcoin is a read-uncontrolled, write-uncontrolled database. This enables everyone to add a fresh block into the ledger, which everyone could also read. An accessed-granted blockchain, similar to a centralized database could be read-controlled and write-controlled. The protocol or the network can be established so only authorized users could add new entries in the database or read the whole database.

But if trust is not an issue and confidentiality matters most, blockchain databases have no actual advantage over conventional databases with centralized administration.

Adding a concealment system to the blockchain will require complex cryptography, and this calls for more computational power for the network nodes. The best way to do this is to just completely hide the data in a private database, which does not even require connecting with the network.

The Challenges Facing Bitcoin

Bitcoin is about to become a decade-old digital currency, but it has still a long way before it can be accepted by the general public. As a matter of fact, the challenges that this cryptocurrency is facing today are quite the same that it has experienced when it was still in its introductory phase.

When Bitcoin was first released, the primary hindrance was the computer skills and understanding of the blockchain jargon required to scrutinize the platform itself. This revolutionary technology involves solving complex algorithms for verification of transactions, which was quite difficult for a layman to chew.

Since then, the Bitcoin's disruptive features made it enticing for users of the underground market or those who are using the Dark Web. Bitcoin became a popular currency for illegal transactions such as criminal activities like drug deals and money laundering.

As a result, Bitcoin was placed in a bad light, which was worsened by the fact that it can be difficult for government agencies and financial authorities to monitor the transactions in the Bitcoin's blockchain. While some governments such as China have issued an outright ban for Bitcoins, other governments such as Japan and the United States still made their due diligence to understand how this cryptocurrency works.

The price volatility also added another layer of challenge for people to accept Bitcoin as payments. In order for widespread adoption to occur, Bitcoins should be stable, should be usable, and should be easily accessible by the general public.

Some advocates believe that there must be changes in the Bitcoin ecosystem in order to capture the mainstream users. For once, the concept should be simplified to earn the public's trust and interest. At present, around 90% of the global population are still not aware of the existence of the Bitcoin.

Why Hackers are Using Bitcoin

Just recently, the series of attacks on private serves has stirred again a long-time discussion on the vulnerabilities of virtual currencies. Just in case you are still not aware, a dangerous malware has been released and spread over 150 countries around the world. The mechanism of the ransomware attack was quite simple. A personal computer will be infected with a virus, which will encrypt files until the owner pays a certain amount as ransom.

In the recent attacks, the people behind the ransomware are asking victims to pay $300 in Bitcoins. And it doesn't end there. If the victim does not pay after three days, the ransom will be doubled, and after seven days and no payment has been received, all the files will be deleted from the computers.

Meanwhile, there is no actual guarantee that the files will be restored again and will be safe if the victim pays the ransom.

The involvement of Bitcoin as a mode of paying the ransom again placed this digital currency in bad light. It becomes an easy tool for hackers because of its special features as a virtual currency. In sending money over digital channels, you can either use your credit cards or online banking, which is linked to your personal information such as your name and address.

But this is not the case with Bitcoin. All the dealings you make via this currency can be concealed. Remember, when you choose to trade in BTCs, a private key that is linked to your wallet will be used to create an encrypted code. This code will be publicly linked with the transaction but not with the people behind the dealings.

Hence, each deal is recorded in a public ledger, which anyone could access and check. Security experts believe that among the possible reasons why hackers and cybercriminals are using BTC as a mode of payment is because it is designed to conceal identity.

In the past, hackers preferred PayPal for their unscrupulous transactions, but because of stricter guidelines in using online platform such as PayPal, they now prefer Bitcoins.

Chapter 3 Quiz

Please refer to Appendix C for the answers to this quiz

1. Why is cryptocurrency difficult to fake?

    A) Cryptocurrency is actually very easy to fake, which is why it is associated with illegal purchases.

    B) Transactions can be reversed, which means the system will kick back fake Bitcoins.

    C) Personal ID is required to transfer coins, so faking a coin would out their identity.

    D) Cryptocurrencies are digital and use cryptographic technology to add a layer of security for the transfer process and record keeping.

2. What is Blockchain?

    A) A distributed ledger that virtually records all transactions of a cryptocurrency such as Bitcoin

    B) A series of blocks chained together in a line

    C) A method of acquiring Bitcoin

    D) A private record of transactions that only Satoshi Nakamoto can access

3. Why are problems linked with Bitcoin?

    A) The underlying framework is faulty

    B) Bitcoin itself is an unreliable digital currency

    C) Users are confused about how Blockchain works

    D) Human error and unscrupulous activity

4. How often does the Blockchain network run automatic checks and balances?

A) Every 3 seconds

B) Once per day

C) Every 10 minutes

D) Whenever a transaction occurs

5. What is a node?

A) A device used in electricity distribution

B) A computer linked to the blockchain network via a client that confirms and relays transactions

C) A computer that stores all information of a cryptocurrency, including private keys

D) A place where users can buy, sell, and exchange their currencies

6. How are node operators rewarded?

A) With Bitcoins

B) With faster transaction speeds

C) With better exchange rates to fiat currencies

D) Node operators are not rewarded

7. What is the most common Graphical User Interface (GUI) created for the blockchain?

A) Windows

B) Android

C) Digital Wallet Apps

D) iOS

8. What does Blockchain technology offer that a centralized database does not?

A) A real-time image of information

B) Nearly unbreakable security

C) Verification of transactions without a third-party

D) All of the above

9. True / False: Blockchain technology is faster than transaction structures such as Visa and Paypal.

Bitcoin

Mining Bitcoin

Chapter 4

Bitcoin Mining

If dollar bills are printed and pennies and quarters are minted, Bitcoins on the other hand are "mined". The process of mining adds transactions to the blockchain as well as to release new digital currencies. This also involves the compilation of recent transactions into the blocks then solving complicated computational problems. Whoever solves the problem will have the incentive of adding the next block on the blockchain and will receive new Bitcoins. This incentivizes mining and involves both the transaction charges (paid to the miner in Bitcoin form) as well as the newly generated Bitcoin.

You can send and receive BTCs over the network. But unless someone could keep a record of these transactions, no one can monitor who had paid what. The blockchain technology manages this by gathering all the transactions that happened during a specific period of time known as a block. It is the job of the miner to verify these transactions and record them into a public ledger.

The public ledger is composed of a long list of blocks referred to as the blockchain. Anyone can review the transactions made within the Bitcoin network. When a member of the network creates a new block of transactions, it will be linked to the blockchain, which builds an expanding list of all the transactions that ever happened in the network. Everyone in the network will receive the latest version of the blockchain so they are continuously in the loop.

However, the public ledger must be built on trust, and it should be digitally held. The miners are crucial in the blockchain system because we need to make sure that the platform will be intact and not compromised.

Once a block of transactions is generated, miners will confine it via a process. They will access the data within the block, use a mathematical formula, and convert it into a shorter version that is composed of numbers and letters called the hash. This is kept alongside the block at a certain point and at the end of the blockchain.

Hashes are quite interesting, because it is quite easy to create a hash from a group of data similar to a Bitcoin block. However, it is almost impossible to read what the data is all about if you just look at the hash. And although it can be a piece of cake to create a hash from huge volume of information, every hash is one of a kind. If you modify at least one character in a Bitcoin block, the hash will completely change.

In generating a hash, miners are not only using the transactions within a block. They also use other bits of information such as the hash of the preceding block relative to where the new block will be connected.

Because every hash of the block is created using the block's hash that precedes it, it is often referred to as the electronic version of a wax letter seal. This is used to verify that this block, including other blocks that succeed it are genuine, as if anyone tries to make any unauthorized modification, every member of the network will be notified.

If one member tries to alter the block, which has already been added to the blockchain, the hash of the block will be changed. If the network tries to verify the authenticity of the block by using the hash function in the blockchain, it will be easy to find that the hash is quite different from the one that is already linked along with that block in the platform. Hence, the compromised block will be flagged as fake.

Since every hash of every block has an effect in the linking of the next hash, altering a block will also make the hash of the subsequent block not genuine, too. This will result to a domino effect as other succeeding blocks will also be affected, which will make the platform unusable.

So this is how Bitcoin miners verify the block. They are all in a competition to be the first one to verify the authenticity of the new blocks. They use software that is designed specifically for verifying blocks and for Bitcoin mining. Each time a member of a network is successful in creating a hash, they will be rewarded with 25 BTCs, the system will update the blockchain, and every node in the network will receive the updated copy. This is the incentive to keep mining and to make the transactions verifiable and genuine.

The challenge is that it can be quite easy to generate a hash from a data set because advanced computers are powerful enough to complete the verification process in several minutes. Therefore, the Bitcoin network must increase the level of difficulty, or else everyone in the network will be able to create hundreds of hashes in no time, and all BTCs will be mined in a matter of days. The Bitcoin network makes this more difficult through the concept of proof of work.

In addition, the Bitcoin network will not accept any old hash, and it requires that the hash of a new block look a certain way. It should have a specific number of zeroes at the beginning. You also can't tell what the hash will look like before you create it. When you include a new piece of information in the group, the hash will be completely modified.

In general, Bitcoin miners are not allowed to interfere with the transaction data within the blockchain. However, they are allowed to change the data that they are using in order to generate a hash. They can do this using a nonce, which refers to a randomized piece of information. This is used with the transaction data in order to generate a hash. If the hash does not fit the needed format, the nonce can be modified, and the entire block should undergo hashing again. It may take several attempts to look for a nonce which works, and all the Bitcoin miners in the network may try to do this simultaneously. This is how miners are earning BTCs.

Network Security of Bitcoin

Because of its decentralized trait, anyone with a reliable internet connection and decent hardware can participate in the blockchain. The network security of Bitcoin will depend on this decentralized platform because the network can make decisions according to consensus. If there is no agreement on adding a block to the chain, the decision can be resolved through consensus. That is, if more than half of the mining power agrees.

If an organization or an individual person has control of higher than the simple majority of the mining power of the whole network, then it can effectively disrupt the blockchain. The possibility that someone can control the majority of the network and use it to corrupt the platform is regarded as the 51 percent attack. The cost of this attack will greatly depend on how much mining power is required in the network. Hence, the network security of Bitcoin will depend in part on how much mining power you use. Moreover, the level of mining power used in the network will directly depend on the incentives that miners have, which are the transaction fees and the block rewards.

Rewards

Block reward refers to the number of new Bitcoins released when each block is mined. However, this is diminishing because the number of Bitcoins mined goes down by 50% every 210,000 blocks. In 2009, the block reward began at 50 Bitcoins, and it went down to 25 Bitcoins in 2014.. Based on the present protocol of Bitcoin, 21 million is the limit and once this number has been reached, mining will stop.

Currently, the block rewards offer the most incentive for miners. At the present moment, the transactions fees are about 0.3 percent of the mining returns.

Transaction Fees

Because the block reward will decrease over time and will eventually hit zero, there will be less incentives for miners. This is now seen as a significant security threat for the platform, unless the transaction fees will replace the incentives provided by the block reward.

The transaction fees refer to a percentage of the amount of Bitcoin, which is added in a transaction as a reward for miners. The Bitcoin sender will voluntarily pay the transaction fees. It is also voluntary to include a transaction in a block. Hence, users who are sending the transaction could take advantage of the transaction fees in order to provide incentive for miners for faster verification of their transactions. By default, the version of the Bitcoin released by the client has minimum rules.

Level of Difficulty

The level of difficulty in mining Bitcoin depends on the level of effort you put into the process across the platform. The Bitcoin platform automatically changes the difficulty level of mining every 2,016 blocks or around every 14 days. This is based on the protocol established by the software, which is coded to align itself with the objective of maintaining the block discovery rate. If you use more computational power in mining, then the difficulty level will be adjusted to ensure that the mining will be more difficult. The opposite happens if the computational power is eliminated from the network. The difficulty level will be lowered down in order to make the process easier.

The profit of the Bitcoin reward becomes higher if the difficulty level is increased. The more people who participate in the mining, the less lucrative mining is for every miner. The size of the transaction fees, the block reward, and the price of Bitcoin all affect the total payout. However, the more people who are into mining, the lower the reward that each participant may receive.

Coordinated Mining

Miners who discover a solution to the problem first will be paid with mining rewards. The possibility that a miner will be the one to find the solution is equal to the percentage of the mining capacity of the whole platform. Therefore, participants with very low computational power have very low probability of solving the next block.

For example, a mining card that you can buy for around $2,000 will only signify lower than 0.0001 percent of the mining capacity of the network. Because of this very low probability of finding the next block, it may take time before a miner discovers a block, and the flexible level of difficulty could make things worse.

This means that there is always the risk that the miner could never recover their investment. Because of such risk, miners decided to form coordinated mining efforts, which are known as mining pools. These are managed by independent parties who agree to work together and share the proceeds among the members. Miners can benefit from a constant stream of digital currencies beginning the day that they become active in the pool.

Recommended Hardware

You can participate in Bitcoin mining if you have access to a reliable internet connection and you have a hardware designed for solving computational problems in blocks. During the early years of Bitcoin, the mining process was performed via regular CPUs from desktop PCs. As Bitcoin became more popular, miners discovered that Graphics Processing Units or GPUs are faster in mining Bitcoins compared to ordinary CPUs. Hence, GPUs became in demand among Bitcoin miners.

Later on, special hardware was designed exclusively for Bitcoin mining. One example is the Application-Specific Integrated Circuit or ASIC, which was introduced in 2013. Later versions have been released with better efficiency and faster processing capacity. With tighter competition in Bitcoin mining, successful miners are only using highly-developed hardware. In using older ASICs, GPUs, or CPUs, the cost of power is far higher compared to the possible returns.

With the development of more powerful ASICs and more miners entering the field, the difficulty level has skyrocketed. Most of this activity has been rewarded by the significant price increase in Bitcoin that happened in 2013 as well as the speculation that its price will rise in the foreseeable future.

Moreover, there is political capacity inside the Bitcoin platform, which comes with regulating mining power, because this mining capacity will basically provide you the voting power whether to make changes in the platform.

Today, there are many companies that are making hardware for Bitcoin mining. Among the popular ones are Butterfly Labs, KnCMiner, HashFast, and Bitfury. There are also companies that are providing lease for hardware such as CEX.io, CloudHashing, and MegaBigPower.

Power Consumption

Aside from the cost of hardware, electricity takes the biggest share in the overhead cost of Bitcoin mining. Electricity is crucial in running the hardware as well as making sure that the space is well ventilated and cool enough to regulate the temperature.

Several large Bitcoin mining facilities have been built near sources of affordable power. For example, CloudHashing is located in Iceland because of cheap power cost and the cold climate greatly helps in the temperature control. In addition, MegaBigPower, the largest Bitcoin miner in North America, is located at Columbia River WA where power cost is very cheap due to the thriving hydroelectric facilities in the state.

Government Regulation

Even though Bitcoin mining is free from government interference, it is still subject to some aspects of the law, especially taxation. In the US, the Internal Revenue Service (IRS) has issued tax compliance rules on Bitcoin and declared that the revenue from Bitcoin mining can be considered as self-employment income and thus must be subjected to personal income tax.

On the other hand, the Financial Crimes Enforcement Network (FinCEN) also issued a policy based on the US Bank Secrecy Act to clarify that those who are mining Bitcoins are not classified as Money Transmitters similar to the classification of cloud mining services. FinCEN is a special department of the US Treasury that works to collect and analyze data on monetary transactions to combat financial crimes such as terrorist funding and money laundering.

What are the Dangers of Bitcoin Mining?

The early years of mining Bitcoin was usually described as a gold rush. This disruptive technology opened up a whole new field in the financial world that provided freedom from banking dependency and the chance to make a lot of money.

Those who saw the potential in Bitcoin and decided to hit the hills were cryptographers, programmers, and like-minded libertarians. But with the popularity of Bitcoin and thousands of miners digging in the digital hill, is there still gold to be mined?

The reality is, Bitcoin mining has achieved a lot of success from a few early adopters. A specialized industry has reached a massive scale in the financial industry. The chunks of profits were already mined a few years ago, and there are very few blocks to be mined as we are nearing the cap of 21 million BTCs.

And even if there are still enough Bitcoins to mine, only those with powerful hardware and those who have access to affordable electricity can take advantage of Bitcoin mining these days.

While it is still possible to mine for Bitcoins, those who have low-powered setups will soon discover that the investment for upkeep and power is higher than what they could generate through Bitcoin mining.

To put it simply, mining is not lucrative for small-scale operations unless you really have access to a cheap power source. It is also true that even large Bitcoin miners are experiencing threat on their profit margins because of the tight competition. In fact, in 2016 the mining company KnCMiner already filed bankruptcy.

You should also take note that the rate of development in hardware is very fast. At any time, more sophisticated and more powerful mining hardware could be introduced in the market, even though experts believe that we are not hitting the technological peak of developed efficiencies.

Meanwhile, even if you pre-order these hardware, there are also delays caused by customs, shipping or manufacturing. There are also some possible problems such as price crashes, network disconnections, power disruption, and hardware failures.

Bitcoin mining can be considered as a business, and in any kind of business, you should consider these risks. The average freelance Bitcoin miner could struggle to make money or recover the cost of mining hardware as well as power. Becoming profitable might be unlikely given the present situation.

This could still be improved in the near future if ASIC hardware hits the point of diminishing returns. With this, combined with affordable and sustainable electricity, could once again make mining for Bitcoin more profitable for freelance Bitcoin miners.

Bitcoin Cloud Mining

If you are interested in becoming a Bitcoin miner, but you don't want to shoulder the burden of buying hardware, you can try cloud mining as an alternative method. Cloud mining, as the name suggests, uses the cloud to mine the Bitcoin network and earn BTCs in the process.

In general, cloud mining makes use of shared processing power to operate data centers that are located remotely. You only need to have Internet access through a reliable device so you can communicate with the network, manage your Bitcoin wallets, and more.

But there are specific risks when you choose to perform cloud mining, which you must understand first before trying this alternative method.

Cloud mining is recommended for you if you want a quiet operation. If you have experienced traditional Bitcoin mining, you have to survive the constant humming of fans all day to successfully mine BTCs. And because the mining is done remotely, you don't have to shoulder significant expenses for power. Also, you can avoid the problem of dispensing equipment if you are no longer interested in Bitcoin mining.

On the downside, cloud mining is vulnerable to fraud. That is why you must first check the credibility and reliability of the cloud mining service that you are considering using. The profits are also low as the operator will have a share on your mined BTCs to cover their costs of running the system remotely. You also don't have full control in the mining operations, and there are also mining services that usually issue contractual warnings that the operations may cease depending on the Bitcoin price.

Chapter 4 Quiz

Please refer to Appendix D for the answers to this quiz

1. The job of the miner is to _____

   A) Devise new methods to enhance Blockchain technology

   B) Remove Bitcoins from circulation

   C) Verify transactions and record them into a public ledger

   D) Stash Bitcoins for use, much like a bank

2. Hashes are _____

   A) A shortened version of data within a block

   B) An elongated version of data within a block

   C) A false set of information used to protect data

   D) A unit used in encrypting data

3. Miners are rewarded for successfully creating a _____

   A) Bitcoin

   B) Hash

   C) Block

   D) Node

4. How many Bitcoins are rewarded per successful creation?

   A) 1

   B) 5

   C) 10

   D) 25

5. What is a nonce?

   A) A randomized piece of information

   B) The confirmation method of Bitcoin transactions

   C) The range of hashes required for each block

   D) A specific number required to authorize a data set

6. The 51 percent attack is a hypothetical situation occurring when?

   A) When 51 percent of the Bitcoins have been mined

   B) When 51 percent of all Bitcoin users sell their coins simultaneously

   C) When a single entity controls 51 percent of the network

   D) When 51 percent of the world actively uses Bitcoin

7. What is a mining pool?

   A) A place where all mining data is stored

   B) An evenly distributed set of blocks that require hashes

   C) A percent chance that a miner will solve the next block

   D) A group of miners who work together and share mining rewards

8. True/False: For freelancer Bitcoin miners, mining is generally not profitable.

9. An alternative to freelance mining is _____

   A) Cloud mining

   B) Strip mining

   C) Government mining

   D) Rush mining

Bitcoin

How it Works

Chapter 5

How Bitcoin Works

Bitcoins have numerous similarities with other forms of currencies whether digital or traditional. However, the most significant feature is that more and more businesses and individuals are now open to accept Bitcoins as payment. You can now shop at your favorite online store, subscribe to an exercise program through an app, or even buy a pizza using Bitcoins.

But Bitcoins are also quite different compared to conventional currencies. Unlike USD or GBP, Bitcoins are not backed up by the US government or the UK government, respectively. Bitcoins are a totally decentralized form of currency and they are not associated with any type of central banking system or financial authority. This is actually Bitcoin's largest appeal. Rather than being confined into a mechanism that is usually filled with manipulation and greed, Bitcoins thrive in a digital platform run by mathematics and are integrated by smart protocols for encryption.

Nowadays, you can use Bitcoins for many types of actual transactions. In order to do so, you first have to purchase Bitcoins however you like, either via cash, bank transfer, or credit card. Bitcoins will be credited to your Bitcoin wallet, and then you can easily send and receive payments to a seller or a buyer without the need for a usual intermediary like a credit card company or a bank.

In eliminating the third-party in the transaction, you can save a lot of money from banking fees, and the parties in the transaction can also keep their identity concealed. However, these features have both advantages and disadvantages for the parties involved. Consider Bitcoin as the virtual equivalent of a financial transaction.

Receiving or spending Bitcoins can be quite seamless like sending a text message, and you can just use your smartphone or your computer. The simplicity of Bitcoin transactions can really surprise users, because behind the platform there are layers of sophisticated mathematical processes that safeguard the deals to maintain their safety and legitimacy.

When you buy or mine Bitcoins, you can keep them in your digital wallet, which you can use for purchases or just for storage if you want to speculate that BTC prices will increase in the future. You can also choose to cash them out in your local currency. When you choose to keep them in your computer, make certain that you understand that there is no centralized institution that keeps the backup of your Bitcoin balance in your wallet.

Therefore, you need to have your own backup of your Bitcoin balance. It is ideal to keep the record of your Bitcoin account on a storage device such as a flash memory, which you can store in a secure location. This is to prevent losing all your Bitcoins if your hard drive fails and corrupts your Bitcoin wallet. There is no way to recover your Bitcoins if this happens.

Bitcoin transactions are also very fast and not reversible. But because the verification process of Bitcoins should share data about the transaction with the whole network, there are instances that you have to wait for several minutes before completing the transaction.

Another advantage is that it is easy to transfer Bitcoins into any country and avoid paying the high fees in international remittances because there are no national policies governing Bitcoins. And because it is free from government interference, your account can never be subjected to freezing and it has no limits.

Bitcoin Exchanges

Take note that in purchasing Bitcoins, sourcing out from your local area is ideal. A basic Google search will allow you to look for the Bitcoin locations in your state or country. It is crucial that you are aware of the exchanges in your country, because the regulations and legal implications that govern in transacting using cryptocurrencies vary from one country to another.

Most Bitcoin exchanges are accepting conventional currencies, so there is no problem in payments. Just make sure that you read the fine print and read the terms and conditions of service especially in Bitcoin transactions.

Almost all available Bitcoin exchanges are now accepting payments through PayPal, credit cards, bank transfers, wire transfers, cash, or other forms of virtual payments. You can select what is comfortable for you. You just need to ensure that your privacy is protected if you are using credit card. Paying with cash is also considered the safest, even though it entails some effort on your part.

You also have to make certain that the transaction fees charged by the Bitcoin exchange are reasonable and actually not too high compared to other avenues in the market. The fees may vary from one Bitcoin exchange to another, and they change over time. There are also several exchanges that are charging for extra fees aside from the exchange or transaction fees.

Transparent Bitcoin exchanges also normally publish their addresses, and they also typically audit their transactions to easily confirm their reserves. Auditing is a standard practice for the Bitcoin exchange to show that they are liquid enough to cover all transactions. This is also crucial to find out if they are running on a percentage exchange.

The order volume is a good indicator of the strength of a Bitcoin exchange. In general, the order volume is just a list of orders that are presently being handled by the exchange. A higher volume order means that more people are using the exchange and so it has high liquidity. While this is a critical factor to consider, you must take note that a Bitcoin exchange that does not publish its order volume doesn't mean that it is not legitimate. More often than not, the exchange has yet to enable this feature or they just have low volume orders at the moment.

Ensuring that your transactions are completely anonymous could be difficult to achieve in a Bitcoin exchange, unless you are buying from someone via cash or Peer-to-Peer platform. Make certain that you confirm that the Bitcoin exchange that you like to use has a standard KYC or Know Your Customer practice. You might need to share some personal information before you can purchase Bitcoins from these platforms.

Another important factor to consider in choosing a Bitcoin exchange is the fulfillment time or the time you can receive your Bitcoins after you buy them. Make certain to also confirm if the platform is offering fixed prices, which means that the purchase price is the price you are charged if Bitcoins are taking several days to arrive in your wallet. This is crucial considering the extreme fluctuations of Bitcoin nowadays.

It is fairly easy to determine the reliability of the Bitcoin exchange that you are considering through the customer reviews and online feedback that the exchange receives. It is ideal to trust the Bitcoin exchange with a high percentage of positive reviews compared to an exchange with limited web presence.

Finally, you have to make certain that the Bitcoin exchange is safe and secure by checking if the site is an HTTPS site. Also check if the exchange offers secure logins alongside other security measures such as two-factor authentication. Security is a non-negotiable factor to consider in choosing your exchange.

Top Bitcoin Exchanges

Because of the popularity and the high promise of returns for Bitcoin trading or investing, there are now numerous Bitcoin exchanges that you can choose, each offering different terms and payment options. Below are the top exchanges you can use to buy your first Bitcoins. All these options are accepting US Dollars as well as other major currencies or other digital currencies.

a) LocalBitcoins

LocalBitcoins is described as more of a platform and less of an exchange where individual traders and investors from around the globe can connect with each other. You can choose to go to an area-specific page and you can choose who you would like to trade Bitcoins with. It also comes with an escrow system that protects the buyer and the seller until the transaction is complete. This is the best platform if you are looking for direct trading, but you should be wary because there are also reports about scammers lurking in the exchange, some of which are using stolen information and fake bank transactions.

b) Coinbase

Coinbase is among the most reliable exchange platforms for Bitcoins today. It is popular for Bitcoin investors and traders because of its dollar cost averaging method, wherein users can choose to automate their purchase weekly or monthly. It is also known for its simplistic platform for buying and selling Bitcoin. It is also interesting to take note that this exchange is monitoring all transactions for dubious accounts and may even close accounts without prior notification.

c) BitQuick

As the name implies, BitQuick offers fast transactions. The platform operates like LocalBitcoin, because you can also buy and sell Bitcoins directly from individuals. There is a 2% fee when buying Bitcoins with BitQuick, while selling is free. You can use this exchange if you are looking for speedy transactions. Shop around if speed is not a deal breaker.

d) Kraken

Kraken is an exchange that specializes in trading Bitcoins. It is popular among Bitcoin traders because it is possible to leverage and even short using the exchange. It also enjoys an outstanding reputation in the financial markets, and is one of the first exchanges to pass an audit from an independent firm. Make sure that when you use this exchange, you know how to set up two-factor authentication as there were reports of accounts being drained when users ignored this security feature.

e) BitStamp

BitStamp is now five years old and the first exchange to be a licensed operator by Bitcoin. It is a preferred exchange because of the platform's ability to process payments using credit cards. There is also an option to withdraw Bitcoins as actual gold, which is a unique selling point of this exchange. Choose this platform if you are searching for a reliable Bitcoin exchange. Also take note that the company is monitoring transactions for dubious activities and will close suspected accounts without prior notice.

f) OK Coin

OK Coin is a Bitcoin exchange company that is popular among traders and investors. It is a non-winner when it comes to the aesthetics of the platform, but it is known for its practical features. This is recommended for traders with enough experience and decent expertise in using the tools and platform for Bitcoin trading.

g) BTC-e

BTC-e is known for its transparent transactions. It is possible to see a live tracker with the prevailing Bitcoin rate as well as the most recent transactions in the platform from the trade's history. It also comes with a chatbox, where users can talk with each other. This unique feature will allow you to learn from industry insights as well as the current sentiments of Bitcoin traders and investors.

h) Circle

Circle is a visually-stunning Bitcoin exchange and ideal for casual Bitcoin users. This is promoted as a user-friendly payment channel that comes with chat functionality. You can also link your credit or debit card to send money to your family and friends through blockchain. Use this channel if you are only looking for a funds transfer solution instead of investing in Bitcoin for long-term.

i) ItBit

ItBit is a trading platform where you can buy and sell Bitcoins. This exchange provides reasonable prices for Bitcoins, but take note that there is a minimal fee. This exchange is also known for offering specialized services for trades that are more than 100BTC. However, this exchange may not be the best platform for you if you are looking for small Bitcoin trades.

j) E-Coin

This Bitcoin exchange platform is popular among those who buy Bitcoins using their debit cards. I have also included this in our list because the exchange allows you to purchase Bitcoin through PayPal, which is rare. While you can also purchase Bitcoins using PayPal through VirWox or Paxful, they carry higher charges.

Choosing a Bitcoin Wallet

After choosing the most suitable exchange for you, the next step is to find a Bitcoin wallet where you can keep your purchased Bitcoins. Because you are investing your money into Bitcoin, selecting the most appropriate wallet for you is an essential step. There are many available wallets today, including the official wallet of the Bitcoin network.

But before choosing your wallet, we first need to discuss the factors that you must consider. Bear in mind that these are my only recommendations so you can make a smart decision in Bitcoin investing. The situation may change based on the market conditions and the stability of your chosen wallet. However, you will be more successful if you do your due diligence first.

a) Transparency

Is the Bitcoin wallet you choose transparent in who they are and how they operate? Check if the site's code is open source. If not, it can be difficult to ensure that the wallet is really secure. Open-source code could be independently checked for vulnerabilities. Also, try to find out if the site's source code is updated.

b) Wallet Security

Ensuring that the wallet you choose is safe to use is crucial. Take note that if you are using a web wallet, you must always be certain that the website is using a secure protocol or HTTPS. Also check if the wallet is using strong logins such as two-factor authentication.

c) Privacy

Is privacy crucial for your Bitcoin investments? Is there a need for you to register before you can use the wallet? Does your chosen exchange accept minimal registration details before you can use it? Does the site use user-verification process such as Know Your Customer (KYC)? These are among the most important things to take note of before you decide.

d) User Experience

Try to determine if the wallet is easy to use or takes some effort. Ideally, you must choose a wallet that is simple and does not require too much mastery before you get started. You should also consider how you will use your Bitcoin, too. A wallet that is specifically designed and optimized for mobile devices can be ideal if you are on the go. But if you are a bit advanced, you can try using a full Bitcoin client directly on your computer. There are also other options that may include hardware devices, so you can store your Bitcoins even if you are not connected online.

e) Multisignature

Aside from securing the wallet, also check if it offers a multisignature option. This is an ideal option if you want your Bitcoin to be safe from online hackers. Multisignature refers to the requirement of more than one key access before you can use the site. This is like opening a box that requires two people with two separate keys to open the box.

f) Backup

Backing up your data is also an essential aspect of Bitcoin wallets. Does the digital wallet that you are considering offer a way to back up your data? Does the platform offer data encryption? Is there a backup restoration process and can you use it without too much effort? Try to explore these options before you load your purchased Bitcoins to your wallet.

g) HD Wallets

Try to find digital wallets that are already HD or Hierarchical Deterministic, which use new Bitcoin addresses to increases user privacy. Privacy is an important concern in Bitcoin investing, and HD wallets carry advanced security features because of their well-rounded infrastructure.

h) Control

Technically, you don't have any control over your wallet if you don't have the access to the private keys. This is a vital factor to consider when you are selecting a Bitcoin wallet. You must have the ability to access your wallet so you have control over your purchased digital currency. This will allow you to move your wallet anytime, and back up your data.

Take note that Bitcoin transactions cannot be reversed. In order to send or spend Bitcoins, you should have the private and public keys. Protecting your private key is your responsibility.

Types of Bitcoin Wallets

There are several types of Bitcoin wallets and they offer different levels and processes for security to make sure that the private keys are protected. Basically, there are five categories of Bitcoin wallets: desktop, online, paper, mobile, and hardware. Some categories may overlap or use hybrid solutions. We will discuss each category and the example of available wallets.

a) Desktop Wallet

Desktop wallets are regarded as the best type of wallet if you are looking for secured storage of Bitcoin. You need to download the software into your desktop PC or laptop and complete transactions using the software, which may not be practical for people who are always on the go. It can also be confusing for beginners in Bitcoin Investing. Below are the top examples of desktop wallets:

i) Armory

Armory is a popular desktop wallet because it is regarded as the only open-source wallet with multi-signature support and cold storage. The private keys will be kept in an offline desktop, so only you will have access to the keys.

ii) Bitcoin Core

This Bitcoin wallet is regarded as the first and original digital currency wallet. It provides you control over your private and public keys that guarantees safe storage. The major downside is that the software requires substantial disk space because it carries the data on each transaction you perform. You have to allocate at least 65GB of free space before you can download the wallet, and you must take note that this space requirement will increase over time as you perform Bitcoin transactions.

iii) Multibit

Compared to Bitcoin Core, Multibit only requires 30MB for downloading. Most Bitcoin traders and investors are using this wallet together with

KeepKey (you will learn more about this later), which is a flash drive that will request manual verification before a Bitcoin transaction could be completed.

b) Online Wallets

Online Bitcoin wallets can be accessed via the Internet using any device if you are connected online. These wallets are easier to use because of their accessibility. However, they are more vulnerable to attacks such as malware, phishing, and hacking. In fact, the meltdown of online wallets such as Bitfinex and Mt. Gox make Bitcoin investors and traders wary of this category.

Even though the Bitcoin online wallets listed below are known for their reliability, it is more ideal to store larger amounts of Bitcoins in other categories of wallets.

i) Blockchain.info

This wallet is regarded as the most popular because around 8 million Bitcoin traders are using this platform to check and process their transactions. This is a winner when it comes to cross-platform capacity, multi-country support, and ease of use. Apart from the online version, Blockchain.info can also be accessed via mobile app and on desktop.

ii) BitGo

A trusted name in the digital currency world, BitGo is regarded as a leader when it comes to securing blockchain technology. This wallet is ideal for individuals and businesses who like fast transactions. More often than not, a Bitcoin transaction requires around three to six verifications that may each take between 30 to 60 seconds. With its zero-verification feature, BitGo allows Bitcoin investors and traders to process fast and secure transactions.

iii) GreenAddress

A lot of Bitcoin traders and investors have the habit of checking their Bitcoin wallets several times per day to ensure that their money is still intact. Frequent logins, especially if performed in unsecured Internet connection will make the account vulnerable to phishing or malware attacks. GreenAddress offers a watch-only platform that can help you to monitor your Bitcoin balances without the need to log in every time you want to check your account.

c) Paper Wallets

Paper Bitcoin wallets are generally safe against online attacks because the Bitcoins are stored offline. You can control your digital currency anytime as you also protect your private keys. The primary disadvantage of using paper wallets is the storage. Paper can be easily lost, torn, or fade. There is also no way to recover paper wallets, so the money could be lost forever if you don't remember the private keys. This is an important factor to consider if you want to use paper wallets.

i) BitcoinPaperWallet

Using this platform, you can print paper wallets that are tamper-resistant. This wallet is also popular among Bitcoin traders and investors who are advocating for cold storage. The website also provides additional safety tips and supplies needed by Bitcoin traders and investors.

ii) BitAddress

BitAddress offers a no-nonsense service, which allows you to produce Bitcoin paper wallets within a matter of minutes.

d) Mobile Wallets

Mobile Bitcoin wallets are practical to use and quite accessible. Many Bitcoin investors and traders are using extra layers of security to make sure their investments will not be wiped out by malicious attacks. It is often recommended to store Bitcoins for trading, while keeping your Bitcoin investments in more secured wallets.

i) Mycelium

Mycelium is known as one of the safest and most popular wallets available for secure storage of Bitcoin on mobile. Often promoted as a bank-grade wallet, Mycelium is categorized as an HD wallet with great features such as watch-only mode and deletion of private keys.

ii) Wirex

This mobile Bitcoin wallet offers both online and mobile wallet services. It is popular among Bitcoin investors and traders because it is safe and easy to use. You can use multi-signature and enable two-factor authentication for both the app and your login on the platform, which makes it extremely difficult for third-parties to access your account.

iii) Xapo

Popular for its secured mobile vault, Xapo integrates multi-signature technology and cold storage to ensure that the Bitcoins are protected from malicious attacks. Its actual servers are located in the Alps and contained in reinforced concrete walls with steel blast doors.

e) Hardware Wallets

Hardware wallets are often used by Bitcoin investors to store their high quantity of Bitcoins. Most hardware wallets are portable and easy to use. They also come with plug and play features that provide users complete control of their Bitcoins.

i) Trezor

Trezor is a reliable name and receives positive feedback online. It is well praised for its simplicity and no-nonsense features. It also comes with extra layers of security to prevent malware attacks and phishing. Its major advantage is the ability to recover Bitcoins in case of loss or theft.

ii) Ledger Nano

This is regarded as the smallest yet the most cost-effective solution in Bitcoin storage. It is about the size of a USB with several variations, commonly the Ledger Nano and the Ledger Nano S. The latter can also contain Ether—another promising digital currency.

iii) Keepkey

Among the biggest fear of a Bitcoin investor is to be attacked by an unknown user that may try to wipe out all their Bitcoin investments. KeepKey helps in preventing this from happening. You need to use the KeepKey device to manually approve every outgoing BTC transaction. Your private keys can be stored in the device, which is also protected by a PIN in case it was stolen.

Learning all of these new things could be overwhelming especially for beginners like you. You might also have second thoughts because you read several news articles about

Bitcoin investors who lost all their money due to malware, hacks, phishing, or just because of human error.

I recommend keeping your Bitcoins in hardware wallets or paper wallets, and if you have the resources, dedicate a high-powered computer so you can accommodate the space requirements of Bitcoin Core. If you prefer keeping your Bitcoins in mobile or online wallets, you may choose to spread them around on reliable websites such as those that are mentioned in this Chapter.

Chapter 5 Quiz

Please refer to Appendix E for the answers to this quiz

1. Which of the following can you NOT do with Bitcoin?

    A) Buy a pizza

    B) Pay your taxes

    C) Shop at an online store

    D) Subscribe to an exercise program

2. True / False: A centralized institution keeps record of all Bitcoin balances, so you can recover Bitcoins from lost accounts.

3. What is the best method to storing Bitcoins for long-term security?

    A) External storage device

    B) Online wallet

    C) Computer hard drive

    D) Online exchange

4. What does a transparent Bitcoin exchange typically do frequently?

    A) Post on social media

    B) Send promotional e-mails to customers

    C) Audit their transactions

    D) Charge high fees

5. BitQuick is an exchange that specializes in _____

    A) Security

B) Transparency

C) Local transactions

D) Speed

6. BTC-e is known for _____

   A) Security

   B) Transparency

   C) Local transactions

   D) Speed

7. LocalBitcoins specializes in _____

   A) Security

   B) Transparency

   C) Local transactions

   D) Speed

8. What is most important to have when storing Bitcoins?

   A) Your Private Key

   B) Your Public Key

   C) An online wallet

   D) An even number of Bitcoins

9. What is the biggest downfall of paper wallets?

   A) They can't store over a certain number of Bitcoins

   B) They aren't conveniently online

   C) They can't store your private key

D) They can be easily lost, torn, or fade

10. While Bitcoin Core is a great desktop wallet, why is it less popular than other options?

    A) It does not offer a user-friendly interface
    B) The user must allocate over 65GB of space for installation
    C) It publicizes the data on each transaction made
    D) The user must give Bitcoin Core their identifying information to download it

Bitcoin's

Record Breaking Price

Chapter 6

Bitcoin's Record-Breaking Price

We have comprehensively explored the history of Bitcoin in Chapter 1. For now, let us discuss the highlights of its timeline to focus on the price fluctuations of this cryptocurrency.

When Bitcoin was created in 2009, no one, not even its early adopters, could have thought that it would experience a massive popularity that it is enjoying today. Its early price was only a measly $0.001 for every BTC. During the next five years, no significant events were recorded, which caused a slow price movement with minimal fluctuations.

In 2013, the banking crisis in Cyprus exploded, which has attracted a lot of attention to Bitcoin. Also in the same year, thousands of people in China began buying Bitcoins in massive quantities, which has resulted to a price increase of about 1000%. But this price surge did not last long.

Mt. Gox, the largest Bitcoin exchange of its time, was attacked. Its share of 60% Bitcoin transactions were compromised, and so the price of Bitcoin plummeted by 40%. It was only until the early months of 2015 that Bitcoin's price was able to recover.

It was in 2015 that Bitcoin started to gain popularity gradually but with stability, and during this year, the price started to rise bit by bit.

From then on, this digital currency has earned the trust of retailers and consumers, which caused its price to enjoy unprecedented increase. It reached its record-breaking price of $4,703.21 in August 2017.

What are the factors that influence the price of Bitcoin?

Several factors affect the price of Bitcoin. This includes of course market demand and supply, the total amount of Bitcoin and Bitcoin owners, technical issues, volatility, geopolitical events, and even news.

The largest factor that is affecting the price of Bitcoin is the *market demand and supply*. Remember, Bitcoin is not represented by any physical equivalent in the brick-and-mortar world. Hence, they are sold on cryptocurrency exchanges. The primary concept in economics dictates that if consumers are buying a commodity, its price will increase, and if consumers are selling a commodity, its price will fall. Bitcoin can be considered as a commodity, and therefore subject to the law of supply and demand. In 2013, the price of Bitcoin surged because of the demand in Cyprus and China.

Another factor that has an impact on the price of Bitcoin is the total amount of Bitcoin and Bitcoin owners. The market cap of Bitcoin is set at 21 Million BTCs, but these are generated with time and effort through mining.

At present, there are around 16 million BTCs in circulation and around 14 million people have their Bitcoin wallets. These figures are increasing fast and because the number of Bitcoins is capped, its price will continue to follow an upward direction.

Everyone can access the blockchain platform that runs the Bitcoin ecosystem thanks to its open-source code. However, repair of some bugs as well as rolling out new updates could lead to an impetus for price fluctuation. Furthermore, massive server attacks or account hacks could bring down the price of this digital currency. Take note that in 2016, Bitfinex's security was compromised after some hackers discovered some vulnerabilities in the system. This has caused another downfall in the price of Bitcoin.

Volatility could also affect the price movement of Bitcoin. Volatility refers to the fluctuation of price over time. It also refers to the level of risk or uncertainty in the value of a security. Higher volatility means that the value of security could also possibly thin out over wide value range. To put this simply, the security price could move dramatically over a course of time in any direction. At present, Bitcoin's volatility is around 10% and it is following a downward curve.

In our ever-connected modern world, a significant event in one country could have an impact in the whole world. One example is the legalization of Bitcoin as an accepted mode of payment in Japan.

Finally, any significant news in the mainstream media related to Bitcoin or the blockchain can have an effect in the price of Bitcoin. This is affected by the human factor involved, which is the way people could respond to news.

Bitcoin's Backing

As you already know, Bitcoin does not have backing from any government or organization. It is not supported by any international agreement and its value is not supported by silver, gold, or any precious metals. But still, Bitcoin has all the traits of a traditional currency.

First, it has uniformity because all BTCs are equal. One Bitcoin is similar to another Bitcoin and they all have the same price and value at any given point in time. Like fiat currencies, Bitcoins are also divisible, because a unit of BTC can be broken down into smaller portions.

Bitcoins are also recognizable because anyone can easily differentiate Bitcoin from other digital currencies. They are also portable as you can easily carry your Bitcoins anywhere you go, and you can also choose to transfer it to anyone you choose. Like actual money, it also carries with it longevity, because Bitcoins will exist in the system and cannot be easily deleted.

And most importantly, Bitcoins are protected from theft and fraud. The primary difference between fiat currencies and digital currencies such as Bitcoin is that the traits described above are guaranteed by protocols, algorithms, and methods supported by mathematics.

Bitcoin Price Volatility

The major volatility in Bitcoin prices were caused by global events, technical issues, and by news in the mainstream media.

a) Global Events

In 2013, several organizations around the world announced their decision to begin accepting Bitcoins as payments. Thousands of Chinese began buying Bitcoins in large quantities and this caused a major rise in the price from $100 to almost $1200. But only after several months, the People's Republic of China announced its ban of Bitcoins in the country, which caused its price to plummet to $500.

b) Technical Issues

The establishment of Mt. Gox was a technological breakthrough in the history of Bitcoin, as the exchange enabled people to cash in Bitcoins to USD. This resulted in the price increase from $0.05 to $1. Four years later, Mt. Gox servers were attacked, which led to a significant price fall.

c) News in the Mainstream Media

Mainstream media covered the release of an updated version of Bitcoin's source code, which resulted in a 10x price increase. In 2011, Time Magazine also published a cover story about Bitcoin focusing on the future of digital currencies. This caused the price of Bitcoin to triple.

Bitcoin Risks and How to Avoid Them

In spite of the amazing returns as well as other possible benefits of Bitcoin, it is still a prevailing fact that this digital currency and the technology that supports it are still considered very young. Basically, there is no guarantee if it will be widely adopted in the future, or it will just become another fad. Its price volatility signifies the uncertainty of Bitcoin's future.

It is important to be aware of certain risks if you wish to trade or invest with Bitcoin.

a) Government Regulation

Government regulation is considered as the highest risk that could affect the future of Bitcoin as an investment instrument. For example, if the US government decides to ban digital currencies including Bitcoin, its price will certainly be affected. The US has the highest number of Bitcoin owners, second only to China. Therefore, any significant shift in regulation will also have a major impact on the price as well as the existence of this cryptocurrency. This is also true with Bitcoin hubs such as UK and Australia. If any major global economy resists cryptocurrencies, the price might collapse, and it could be a difficult struggle.

b) Massive Threats Against Bitcoin Platforms

Another possible risk for the existence of Bitcoin is the possible massive scale attacks on crucial Bitcoin platforms such as exchanges and wallets. Remember, the attack against Mt. Gox in 2014 and BitFinex in 2016 have considerably affected Bitcoin's price. Price records show that since the launch of Bitcoin in 2009, about 30 percent of Bitcoin platforms have been compromised. Despite the efforts to improve the security on these exchanges as well as Bitcoin companies, the risk of massive attack is still there, and there is no guarantee that attacks will be thwarted in the future. But it is also true that many of these attacks only have short-term impact on the price of Bitcoin, and do not really affect the price in the long run.

c) Bitcoin Scalability

Because Bitcoin has no central governing authority, there are important decision points that are not properly addressed. One example is the failure of the market participants to have a consensus on how to deal with scalability issues. To become profitable in Bitcoin investment, the blockchain technology must be able to handle a high volume of transactions, which must be even higher compared to what is processing now. It should also become more dynamic within a limited time period.

At present, Bitcoin transactions require around 30 minutes, which is reasonable and even practical if you are sending money overseas. But this is not recommended if you are trying to pay for a cup of coffee. There are many places where Bitcoins are accepted as payments. But for now, the best thing to do with Bitcoin is to hold it for investment or for trading and not as a tool for exchange in daily transactions.

The core team that manages the Bitcoin platform has already presented some ideas to improve the scalability of this digital currency, and most of them are now under testing. If they are successful, they will move on to adaptation. However, the majority of Bitcoin participants should reach a consensus and approve the changes before any significant change will be rolled out. Without consensus, Bitcoin's scalability can be a challenge, and could even result in Bitcoin struggling as a currency for everyday transactions.

d) Trading Difficulty

While there are numerous exchanges today that are providing services for Bitcoin trading, it is not easy to facilitate money transfer from your PayPal account to your Bitcoin wallet. But it seems that this will improve in the short while, as more companies will be established to fill this gap.

e) 51 % Attack

Not everyone, even those who own Bitcoins, is aware of the possibility of a 51% attack. This threat refers to a centralized Bitcoin mining operation that could take more than 50 perent of the blockchain, and at which point it could have the power to reverse transactions, and therefore make the entire platform unusable as participants might not trust the exchange anymore. At present, the Bitcoin network is totally decentralized, and mining operations are running around the globe. If one mining company acquires control over the blockchain, Bitcoin's future as the currency of the future could be compromised.

f) Emerging Cryptocurrencies

There is a possibility that the world may embrace the concept of cryptocurrencies or the blockchain technology, but not necessarily Bitcoins. There is always the risk that other emerging digital currencies could overtake Bitcoin and take its place as the main cryptocurrency. As we have mentioned earlier, the current Bitcoin technology has some challenges such as scalability, which could be improved by rising cryptocurrencies.

However, it is also true that Bitcoin has managed to grab its first-mover advantage, and its expanding ecosystem results in its strong position as the leading cryptocurrency that may dispel this risk. Furthermore, research also shows that the Bitcoin price will be more valuable compared to other rising cryptocurrencies. Hence, if you are interested in investing in this digital currency, you may make a serious profit if you hold your Bitcoins for a while.

g) Bitcoin's Untraceable Nature

During its early years, and even today, Bitcoin is quite attractive among criminals because the transactions are effectively untraceable. Anyone can go into the drug trade or sell things that can be found in the black market with less risk of being traced by authorities. In this view, Bitcoins are somehow comparable to regular money, which can be used for fraud or crime. This feature can also bring unwanted attention from government authorities that could result in stringent policies in using cryptocurrencies.

Reducing Your Exposure in Bitcoin Trading or Investing

At this point, you should have a general understanding of some risks associated with Bitcoin trading and investing. In order to become profitable in this cryptocurrency, you should be aware of common ways to reduce your exposure to risk.

a) Protect Your Bitcoins from Counterparty Risk

While the cryptocurrency market provides the best gains at the present, there are still risks that you must manage and Bitcoin exchanges come with a certain level of counterparty risk. Take note that Bitcoin transactions cannot be reversed, and they trust an exchange with your private keys that could lead to significant losses.

As crypto traders or investors, there is no sure way to eliminate counterparty risk. However, there are certain steps that you can follow to considerably reduce the risk. This includes learning more about the Bitcoin exchange to ensure that it is a reliable platform, diversifying your BTCs across several exchanges, and investing at least 70 percent to 80 percent of your portfolio, then protecting the rest of your assets. Also, you must never leave your BTCs in an exchange if you will not be active in trading for a while.

b) Focus on Quality over Quantity

Those who are trading or investing in Bitcoin have the tendency to waste too much time and money. Take note that the key to profitable trading is to focus on quality instead of quantity. Not every type of market condition is ideal for your strategy. For instance, scalping can be more effective if the Bitcoin market shows some stability. On the other hand, swing trading can be ideal if the trends indicate some strength. To be sure that you are investing in quality trades, you must first figure out your trading style and also learn how you can spot the right Bitcoin market conditions.

c) Avoid Investing or Trading Motivated by Hype

Traders and investors have to manage the fear of missing out or losing on a good trade or investment. Panic selling could lead to cashing out your investment too early, while giving in to your greed could result to losing your investment. It is crucial to learn how you can manage your emotions and remain objective if you are engaging in Bitcoin investing.

Usually, when the hype is at its peak, the situation could be that the market may reach into the distribution phase, which will be followed by a downtrend. News alerts from primary media outlets could be too late, as they will only release the report on the emerging trends once they have verified that the market is not overhyping. Make certain that you manage to get in before the rest of the pack, then sell your units when the hype reaches its climax.

d) Don't Use Too Much Leverage

Bitcoin traders and investors often use margins because they have to expand the order size and offer the flexibility of going long or short. Hence, when you are using too much leverage, you may not have sufficient time to absorb all the relevant information and you may end up losing a sizeable portion of your capital when the unit liquidates automatically.

Some exchanges are providing leverages as high as 100 percent, but in this case, even a one percent move against your investment could easily eat up your whole account. A recommended strategy is to find an exchange that offers a triple leverage that will allow you to earn triple gains while still maintaining a decent amount of buffer so you can easily exit a bad trade. But you may not do this when you are scalping time frames if the markets become too volatile. In general, the longer that you hold the trade, the less leverage that you can use.

e) Planning Your Exit

Be sure that you are aware of the key resistance and support levels on your Bitcoin investment plan and map out your trades as early as you can. Also make certain that you are aware of the risk-reward ratio and set your targets for exiting the trade. As a Bitcoin investor, you may add your position if the trends show positive indicators, or choose to fix your profits if you are scaling out. Moreover, you must make certain that you have already established your stop orders to protect yourself if the markets are moving against you. Just remember that the stops are not 100% effective if the price fluctuation is happening too fast, and you may even end up experiencing some losses as a result of market corrections.

The Future of Bitcoin's Price

There is no sure way to know what will happen in the future as any currency, digital or fiat, is subject to collapse. Many currencies have lost their values in the past including the Zimbabwean Dollar or the German Papiermark. In a very short period of time, their prices dramatically plummeted to zero. They became obsolete because the prices of services and goods increased significantly.

In the case of cryptocurrencies such as Bitcoin, geopolitical events, code problems, and technical limitations are possible deal breakers. Nonetheless, at present, there are no impending symptoms of Bitcoin's devaluation.

Many advocates of digital currencies as well as financial and investment experts believe that the current platform of Bitcoin is not a bubble, and its growth is stable.

Bitcoin is considered as a young currency, which means it has great growth potential. It is difficult to project the price movement of Bitcoin, so to stay updated on the current and forthcoming trends, you should always tune in to related news about cryptocurrency and be alert in the price fluctuations.

Chapter 6 Quiz

Please refer to Appendix F for the answers to this quiz

1. The starting price for one Bitcoin in 2009 was:

    A) $.01
    B) $1
    C) $.0001
    D) $10

2. Which is NOT a factor in Bitcoin's price?

    A) Geopolitical events
    B) Market demand and supply
    C) News
    D) Inflation

3. What is the market cap for BTCs?

    A) 21 million
    B) 11 million
    C) 31 million
    D) Infinite: unlimited Bitcoins can be mined

4. What is Bitcoin backed by?

    A) Bitcoin is not backed by anything
    B) Gold
    C) Silver
    D) Fiat currencies

5. In 2013, after several organizations announced Bitcoin as a form of payment, what happened?

   A) The price of Bitcoin crashed as users did not trust these agencies
   B) Norway's GDP nearly doubled due to Bitcoin transactions
   C) The price of Bitcoin surged due to thousands of Chinese buyers
   D) Japan banned the currency after seeing its volatility

6. What is the highest risk that could affect the future of Bitcoin?

   A) Scalability
   B) Government Regulation
   C) 51% attack
   D) Altcoins

7. True / False: Any currency, digital or fiat, is subject to collapse.

8. Without _____, Bitcoin's scalability will be a great challenge.

   A) Consensus
   B) Legislation
   C) Centralization
   D) Argument

Bitcoin

Is It the Right Investment for You?

Chapter 7

Is Bitcoin the Right Investment for You?

Prior to exploring the factors which can guide you to determine if Bitcoin is the right investment vehicle for you, it is crucial to understand the difference between trading and investment. Even if you have basic investing knowledge, it is ideal to review these concepts in the context of Bitcoin investing.

In general, trading and investing are two different strategies to make money through financial instruments. The main use of investing is to accumulate wealth over time by buying and holding bonds, equities, currencies, and other financial vehicles.

As an investor, you can make more money through compounding or via the process of reinvesting the profits as well as dividends into more shares. The investments are normally held in a timeframe that may range in weeks, months, or even years. You can also take advantage of the added benefits in investments such as interest and dividends.

But like other financial markets, the price of Bitcoin can still fluctuate, so investors can ride out the risk with the possibility the price could soon recover and any loss could be easily restored. You can also refer to market fundamentals in searching for investments such as managing price-earning ratios as well as forecasts.

Meanwhile, trading is mostly about regular buying and selling financial vehicles like currency pairs, stocks, and commodities. The main purpose of trading is to make profits that could outperform investments. If you are active in trading, you can aim for at least 10% profit each month in comparison to a potential 10% profit of an investor, which may take longer to materialize.

The profits that you can earn from trading are basically sourced out from purchasing instruments at a lower rate compared to selling them at a higher price in a shorter time period. In addition, it is also possible to make profits through selling financial instruments if the price is higher than purchasing to cover if the price falls down. This is known as selling in short order to make profits in spite of the downward trends in the market.

Investors are usually patient to wait out the possibility of less profitable scenarios, while traders are familiar with taking losses or profits within a shorter period of time. Traders also use protective stop loss orders to easily manage in dealing with losing positions at a pre-existing rate. Traders are also adept in using different tools for technical analysis like moving averages and stochastic oscillators to search for the trading setups with high potential in order to make profits.

Because cryptocurrencies such as Bitcoin are now treated as financial instruments, you can now make profits through trading or investment. Bitcoin traders normally take advantage of the price fluctuations to make profits, while investors are looking for higher returns over a certain period of time through buying and then holding the cryptocurrency.

After gaining a basic understanding of the differences between investing and trading, the next step is to explore the various factors that could help you decide if Bitcoin is the best financial investment for you.

Why Trade or Invest in Cryptocurrencies Such as Bitcoin?

Investing or trading Bitcoin could be a profitable activity, regardless of whether you are a beginner or an expert in the financial markets. Cryptocurrencies are fairly new, highly volatile, and have wide spreads at the moment. Arbitrage and margin trading are also now quite common, so many individuals are still making profits in investing or trading in Bitcoins.

The so-called "bubble" and the volatility track of Bitcoin has possibly done more to attract additional investors as well as traders compared to any other feature of this digital currency. In every instance of the Bitcoin bubble, it is followed by a hype for this cryptocurrency that makes it even more popular. This publicity results in a price increase, because more and more traders and investors are having their interest piqued.

For beginners, the Bitcoin platform may be treated as a virtual gold mine, where you can make money anytime and anywhere as long as you have the right software and hardware. But this is far from reality. Many investors and traders often give up after only several weeks of trading or once they suffer significantly after a market crash. They don't understand that this is the essence of Bitcoin as a financial vehicle. It comes with high volatility, and the price could easily fluctuate in only a matter of minutes.

However, it can be rewarding to own a percentage of what is known as the currency of our future. The main idea here is that you must first understand the key element of Bitcoin, which includes its similarities to conventional financial instruments and its uniqueness as a digital currency.

Bitcoin is considered as a breakthrough creation, because it is one of a kind, and the world has not seen a successful digital currency, despite the fact that there were already earlier versions of virtual cash systems prior to 2009. But nowadays, Bitcoin is just one — but the most popular — of the hundreds of digital currencies (called altcoins), which are all using the blockchain technology of cryptography to manage the production and to transfer value.

In the previous chapters, we have already discussed the advantages of the Bitcoin exchange over the present-day conventional fiat system. It is known for its decentralized system, so there is no need for an independent party or a central authority to manage the transfer. Therefore, it is possible to send money to anyone regardless of the time zone or location. This discards the need for traditional firms such as wire transfer companies or banks. In addition, the system also gets rid of the need to pay added fees or wait for several days for the money to be available in your bank account. Through the Bitcoin platform, transfer of value (cash) can be facilitated within a few minutes.

The Nature of Bitcoin as a Financial Instrument

Bitcoin is a breakthrough because of the technology that supports it and the innovative platform that is free from any interference from the government. But before you begin trading or investing Bitcoin, there are several factors that you must understand about the nature of Bitcoin as a financial instrument.

a) Bitcoin Prices Fluctuate Several Times a Day

Bitcoin became popular because of its fast and frequent price fluctuations. High volatility is a common feature of the equities market, which is not an attractive factor for investors, but appealing for traders who want to make profits through price changes.

b) You Can Invest or Trade in Bitcoin Anytime

Bear in mind that the Bitcoin platform is decentralized. There is no official platform where you can exchange Bitcoin. That means there is also no official trading time for this digital currency. Unlike the stock markets with rigid operating hours that exclude weekends, you can still trade Bitcoins anytime and anywhere as long as you have an internet-enabled device (desktop computer, tablet, or smartphone) and a reliable internet connection.

c) Bitcoin Is Not Limited by Geography

Bitcoin is not a traditional currency. Its price is not directly influenced by the policies or economy of one state or government. This digital currency also has a tumultuous timeline before it become a bit stable as a currency, and many of these events are linked with worldwide events.

Bitcoin Investing vs Bitcoin Trading

There's a great difference between investing and trading Bitcoin. Just similar to other conventional financial vehicles, investing money in currency is different than trading in company equities. And in Bitcoin investing or trading, it is crucial that you also learn more about buying digital currencies.

Buying Bitcoins can be easy, but it depends on the wallet and exchange you prefer. But, this is not like purchasing foreign currency if you are overseas. There is no need to follow tedious process, because you just have to search for the right exchange and open your digital wallet, and pay for the cryptocurrency in USD. Therefore, purchasing Bitcoin is quite common among people who just like to try the currency then invest a portion of it or for those who are mere curious about this emerging virtual money.

Meanwhile, investing is part of a long-term strategy, which involves a portfolio that contains different cryptocurrencies, business acumen, and conventional hedging or risk. Usually, investors are not concentrating on the volatility of the cryptocurrency, and they usually not give up easily on the investment during price fluctuations.

Bitcoin trading is often a part of a short-term strategy. Most traders are just trying the market, monitor the trade for several weeks or months, and then sell the units as soon as they think that the price is at its best offer. Hence, Bitcoin traders are quite sensitive to price fluctuations and could easily sell the units when there is a risk of losing.

Bitcoin Trading Risks

While there are risks related to trading and investing Bitcoins, the former has higher exposure because of the vibrant nature of this digital currency. Investors are trained to wait out a market downfall and they normally have the reserved resources to help them cope with the possible losses. Meanwhile, trading is often compared to gambling, because traders should react to the market conditions and they are adept in figuring out the right time to sell. Most of the risk in Bitcoin trading is often linked with the errors of inexperienced traders.

Most Bitcoin exchanges have their own preferred wallets, which you can use to keep your Bitcoins and make the trading easier. But certainly, this is not the safest method. For instance, one of the most popular downfalls in Bitcoin's timeline is the crash of Mt. Gox, which was the largest Bitcoin exchange of its time. Its collapse led to the loss of more than 800,000 BTCs, which have never been recovered.

Clearly, it is best to trade or invest in Bitcoin if you are only using your excess money. Never use your kid's college fund to gamble in this financial market. You must also be careful and only invest in reliable and safe exchanges and wallets. Take note that there is no central authority that regulates Bitcoin. In spite of Bitcoin as a modern platform to expand your wealth, the old rule in investing is still true—never place all of your eggs in one basket.

Bitcoin Trading Capital Risks

If you are looking into Bitcoin trading, you'll have an advantage if you have some sort of background in trading or investing with conventional financial markets. Don't trade or invest in Bitcoin using all your capital, as you must first experience and properly understand the current market for cryptocurrency.

Most beginners are normally disillusioned with the concept of how much they can make from trading Bitcoins. The exchange for cryptocurrency is definitely more vibrant and the rates move faster compared to traditional stock markets. However, this also has higher risk. The fluctuations on the value of fiat currency can be gauged in a small percentage of a dollar, while the Bitcoin rates may fluctuate on extreme ends within a day.

Is it Ideal to Invest or Trade in Bitcoin?

There is no best answer for this question as the most suitable answer will largely depend on your knowledge about the platform as well as the resources available. You can begin investing in Bitcoin with a minimal amount of funds, which you can steadily increase as you learn more about the exchange. This is also a long-term investment strategy, which could gradually yield a large amount of cash. This can also neutralize the high fluctuations of Bitcoin as it will let you understand the market more and avoid large losses.

Meanwhile, Bitcoin trading is usually reserved for those who are more skilled in the depth and nature of Bitcoin, and those who have the luxury of time to monitor the fluctuations, which is crucial to make substantial gains even within a single day.

Chapter 7 Quiz

Please refer to Appendix G for the answers to this quiz

1. What is the goal of investing?

    A) To give away money for the good of everyone

    B) To gamble

    C) To trade with consistent positive margin

    D) To accumulate wealth over time

2. What has the "bubble" and volatility track of Bitcoin done?

    A) Attracted more investors and traders to the market

    B) Dissuaded investors and traders from entering the market

    C) Crashed the price of Bitcoin to near worthless levels

    D) Increased the total market cap of Bitcoin

3. How often do Bitcoin prices fluctuate?

    A) Once per month

    B) Once per day

    C) Once per week

    D) Several times per day

4. Bitcoin is limited by:

    A) Geography

    B) Trading times

    C) Third-party agencies

    D) None of the above

5. What contributes to most of the risk in Bitcoin trading?

   A) Potential for being hacked
   B) Barrier to entry
   C) Inexperienced trader decisions
   D) Volatility in price

6. Is it ideal to invest or trade in Bitcoin?

   A) Yes, there is plenty of profit to be made with little investment or risk.
   B) No, there is little profit to be made with high investment or risk.
   C) The answer largely depends on your personal financial situation and proclivity for risk.
   D) It is too late to invest or trade in Bitcoin.

How To

Make Money In Bitcoin

Chapter 8

How to Make Money In Bitcoin

Trading or investing in Bitcoin has its own set of risk and rewards. It's normal to take extra precautions when investing in a new financial instrument such as digital currencies. However, for the past five years, Bitcoin has surged its median price, and it still seems to have great potential in the next few years. Many early investors in Bitcoin are venture capitalists who want to make profit through their expert foresight.

Investment experts believe that digital currencies such as Bitcoin are now at their peak, and those who have invested early on can reap the rewards of high gains, although this digital currency does not have the same stability and value of traditional currencies. But with the emerging technologies and tools for Bitcoin mining and distribution, there is high potential that more people and businesses will soon embrace this currency.

Establishing Your Bitcoin Investment Plan

Whether or not you are interested in investing or trading Bitcoin, you should always have a plan to be profitable in this emerging financial instrument. Figure out the profit margin for your investment portfolio. Bear in mind that accumulating a retirement fund through Bitcoin investment is quite different compared to day trading this cryptocurrency.

Since Bitcoin prices could easily fluctuate according to the market demand, it is important that you establish a clear goal with practical and realistic values, so you can decide when to invest or trade. This will also guide you in determining the right time to exit or enter the market. Having a plan is quite beneficial and must be the first part of your investing or trading plan.

Bitcoin's Price Fluctuation

It is just common for the price of cryptocurrencies to rise and fall several times in a day or even in an hour. Investors or traders should figure out the reason behind every major fluctuation. Take note that Bitcoin is an emerging currency and very few companies are beginning to accept it as payment. This means that traditional regulations usually don't apply to Bitcoin. In addition, different countries also have different policies about digital currencies. Bitcoin is also highly vulnerable to significant news as the price is closely linked to the market demand. Any minor news that is related to Bitcoin and cryptocurrencies in general could influence its price.

Bitcoin as a Possible Replacement Currency

There is some sort of certainty that the way we pay for goods and services could drastically change, even if Bitcoin becomes successful for only about half of its projection. While many investors recommend the strategy of cautious adoption, there are several Bitcoin features that make the cryptocurrency more appealing compared to traditional currencies.

In general, holding the cryptocurrency will eliminate the charges as well as the policies applied to traditional money. Also, Bitcoin's nature allows immediate transaction that could lead to significant reduction on cash flow delays. Moreover, the transaction is digital so there is a growing concern about security. While traditional financial institutions can keep track and easily discontinue accounts that are involved in fraud, the Bitcoin platform has no central authority to manage the account of a person who lost his or her private keys.

The Novelty Value of Bitcoin

One of the best ways to use this cryptocurrency for business is to accept it as a form of payment. Since Bitcoin is currently considered a novelty, establishments such as the EVR Bar in New York City attracted substantial publicity because it was the first bar in the world to accept BTC payments.

As more businesses and individuals begin to acknowledge Bitcoin as a tradeable and dependable currency, its price could become stable and its value could increase. As an investor, putting money on companies that adopt the Bitcoin technology can be risky, but there is a high reward if everything pans out.

Becoming a Small-Scale Bitcoin Exchanger

Today, the best way to make profit through Bitcoin trading is via an exchanger. You just need to sign up with a peer-to-peer exchange marketplace such as Bitsquare or LocalBitcoins so you can start offering a service in your area for trading Bitcoins.

Adding a spread into every trade will allow you to make some profit. For example, you can offer to buy 2 percent below the current price or sell 2 percent above the current market price. It is best to offer a convenient way for your peers to trade with you. You might even make each deal more personalized. Once you are always available to facilitate a trade, people will come back to you and will be happy to pay the spread.

At first, you should be prompt in completing deals, and you need to respond fast. This will allow you to gain your customer's trust and eventually, you will be known in your area as a reliable and legitimate Bitcoin exchanger.

Becoming a Bitcoin exchanger is usually one of the easiest ways to start making profit in the Bitcoin world, because there is no need for comprehensive financial analysis. Investing or trading in Bitcoin usually requires more knowledge and skill. Day traders often use online exchanges, and often aim to sell or buy based on the projection that the Bitcoin price will fluctuate downwards or upwards.

As a Bitcoin exchanger, you can also offer the service of completing order books that are usually popular among people who are interested in buying and selling cryptocurrencies for practical use instead of holding. You can make profit by simply taking offers as a form of speculating if the price of Bitcoin will rise or fall.

So long as the market doesn't fluctuate that fast, there is always the possibility of making enough income as an exchanger regardless of whether the price is falling or rising. If the market is following an upward trend, then it is best to buy more Bitcoins instead of selling. In this scenario, you can provide an average selling price, then a better buying price, or you can just focus all your efforts in buying. Therefore, as an exchanger, you could increase your profits by being a day trader. Offering exchange services will also provide traders with a safe way to test out the waters.

Even when you are in a centralized exchange where you don't need to directly transact with your customers, you may still make money by offering exchange services. This can be done by making offers rather than taking them.

Once you put the Bitcoin offers in the order books rather than accepting offers that are already there, you can easily gain a better price. Because you are also providing a service, you can assume the role of a market maker even without substantial capitals.

Some Bitcoin exchanges are also providing rewards if you focus on making offers rather than taking offers. These rewards may be in form of Bitcoins or lower exchange costs. Becoming a market maker or a Bitcoin exchanger is one of the simplest ways that you can do to make money in this emerging currency.

A Strategy is Crucial to Make Money in Bitcoin

A well-established strategy is crucial to become profitable in the Bitcoin world. It is important that you are fully aware of what you want when you are opening a trade. This should also include your target profit as well as the loss that you can stand before you exit the market. A well-defined time frame is also another crucial factor to consider as well as a flexible strategy, so you can make necessary changes.

Following the Cryptocurrency Trend

Most financial instruments usually follow long-term price rates, wherein the whole movement is moving in one direction for several months or even years. A clear trend will persist even if the price fluctuates every now and then. Financial markets investors often look for this long-term trend and place their investments based on the trend. In long-term investment, there is no need to determine the point at which a trend could turn and a new one begins in an opposing direction as long as you don't have to withdraw your investments soon. It doesn't matter if it will take you several months to verify a market trend if it usually takes years for an average trend to complete.

Using Fundamental Analysis for Bitcoin Trading or Investing

You are certainly familiar with fundamental analysis if you have a background in the stock market. In investing or trading Bitcoins, you can also use fundamental analysis, which requires you to look at the fundamental data affecting the price of this digital currency. This includes the volume reported by the businesses who already embrace Bitcoins, the number of active wallets, the number of daily transactions, the volume traded on Bitcoin exchanges, and many more. After this, you could use the data to estimate what you think is the actual value of Bitcoin at present. Take note that your decision could depend on whether you think this digital currency is undervalued or overvalued, and then you can trade according to your estimates.

Even though fundamental analysis is a traditional tool used by investors and traders in speculating the different asset classes such as stocks and currencies, some experts in the financial markets believe that using this analysis in evaluating Bitcoin could be a bit complex.

For instance, you can choose to assess the stock of a company by simply looking at certain items in the balance sheet. But for digital currencies, there are no earnings that you can assess. Therefore, it could be a challenge to yield an even remotely precise estimate for the value of Bitcoin if you only depend on the future cash flows the way you assess other assets like Microsoft equities. So, investors and traders who are not convinced of using fundamental analysis to assess Bitcoin prices are now using different metrics.

Even though Bitcoin is considered as a new type of asset class, the same metrics can also be used for evaluating fiat currencies. Moreover, all the economic laws as well as theories can also be applied for digital currencies. Hence, the starting point for all fundamental analysis should be the demand and supply that can also drive the prices.

a) Evaluating Demand for Bitcoin Investing

Trading is one of the factors that affects Bitcoin's demand alongside adoption and transaction activities. Many experts underscore the importance of user adoption, which is essential in the long-term viability of the cryptocurrency. As for what is driving the user adoption, money has various uses.

In essence, money is used as a channel for exchange, an account unit, and storage value. Gradually, Bitcoin is now used as a unit of account beyond special groups. This digital currency also managed to attract significant traction as a medium of exchange. Several companies such as eBay, PayPal and Microsoft have embraced Bitcoin as a mode of payment.

Moreover, the number of daily verified transactions have maintained a stable rising trend. The surge in transactions began in 2012 with more than 7000 daily transactions recorded in April 2012 to an average of 350,000 to 400,000 daily transactions today.

And while this data is regarded as informative, this is not an ideal factor to consider, because there is still a substantial portion of blockchain activities that are generated via automated exchanges and don't really indicate economic activity. Instead, traders and investors must figure out which transactions are made by genuine traders who are actually receiving or sending Bitcoins from other parties.

As Bitcoin attracts more popular adoption and businesses slowly adopt this cryptocurrency, there is also a considerable shift in focusing on Bitcoin as a storage of value and platform of exchange. When perceived as an alternative vessel for containing value, Bitcoin's price can surge high.

b) Evaluating Supply for Bitcoin Investing

While it takes a high level of study to assess the demand of Bitcoin, evaluating the role of supply can be more direct. Remember, the blockchain protocol puts a cap on the number of BTCs at 21 million, and as of now, there are around 16.3 million BTCs that are in circulation.

Furthermore, the Bitcoin platform also specifies the new supply rate, which is in contrast with the traditional currency model in which the central bank has the authority to print money as needed. However, there are also some restrictions that affect Bitcoin's supply.

It is interesting that Satoshi Nakamoto owns around 1.1 million BTCs, which until now have never been accessed. Many experts believe that these BTCs are not used at all and even regard to this volume as dead BTCs. Furthermore, there is no way to figure out the exact number of dead BTCs. This is primarily because during the early days of Bitcoin, BTCs cost peanuts. But when the price began to surge, many people realized that they had thrown away their hard drives containing the private keys, which are required to access their Bitcoin wallets.

c) News Monitoring

Like the foreign exchange and the stock market, the Bitcoin price will fluctuate depending on what is happening in the world. For example, a government announcing a stringent policy on digital currencies, or a major currency under attack by a malware, can affect Bitcoin's price. More liberal policies on financial technology or unicorn companies getting funded through BTCs could drive the price up.

But news monitoring for Bitcoin trading or investing is not a recommended strategy, because there are very few people who have the luxury of time to be always watching for the news and immediately deciding what to do. Quite often, the market has already responded before you can even learn the whole story. And even if you have the time to always watch the news, this is not enough to make a wise investment decision.

Capitalizing on correction is another strategy that you can use to make money out of Bitcoin trading. More often than not, the financial markets have the tendency to respond to hype. There are investors or traders who withdraw from the market without even evaluating the impact of the news. Therefore, a 20% fall, for example, is normally followed by an increase between 5 and 10% as the market tries to correct the overreaction. Once you become adept in this strategy, you can have another way to use news reports to become profitable in Bitcoin trading.

Swing Trading

The profit strategies that we have explored thus far are regarded as medium-term or long-term methods. It may take several months or years before they can provide you actual returns. Some people easily end up with low profit margins, and some also lose their whole investment.

If you want a faster way to make money through Bitcoin, you can try day trading. This profit methodology refers to the process of trading the digital currency over short-term fluctuations of Bitcoin price. The activity usually lasts only for a few days rather than months or years.

Swing trading is the most popular strategy for day trading. This is a method that you could use to figure out the turning points in short-term trends. This often involves searching for support and resistance levels. The former refers to the falling price level, which is projected to meet the resistance as market participants are entering the market to purchase a bargain. Meanwhile, the resistance level signifies a scenario where a rising price move is projected to meet the sellers' resistance who are also making a profit in the market.

Using Technical Analysis for Bitcoin Trading or Investing

Technical analysis is also used by traders and investors in the foreign exchange market or the equities market. This basic investment or trading tool involves the use of chart patterns and mathematical formula to predict the movement of the price in the future.

Unlike fundamental analysis, technical analysis is totally based on the existing data and volume data. Therefore, there is no information about if the price is too high or too low. Rather, technicians (people who are using technical analysis) believe that there are recurring patterns and trends, which will always appear in the market.

Many of these are based on the natural behavior of market participants, which are all but human. They have the tendency to act in a particular way to various price movements. Some investors also believe that the changes in the actual value are affected by the market participants, and so taking a closer look at these actions could provide people with all the information needed to make a wise investment decision.

Chartists (another term used to describe people who believe in technical analysis) are taking a more practical approach in evaluating the history of the asset through price charts, and they are using various analytical tools to understand how the market feels about Bitcoin.

Technical analysis underscores the actual monitoring of the price movement. This is in contrast with fundamental analysis, which focuses more on the worth of a security. In evaluating Bitcoin's price history, you could try to identify usual patterns such as support and resistance. For you to better understand technical analysis, it is important that you become familiar with the basic notions of the Dow Theory, which is mainly used for evaluating securities, and in effect can also be used to analyze Bitcoin price movements.

First, the price movement is not completely random. Instead, they follow specific trends, which could be either short-term or long term. If a unit is following a trend, there is a high chance that it will follow the trend rather than going the opposite direction. Through technical analysis, you can spot on Bitcoin trends and make profit if you correctly predict that there will be a difference in the price if you choose to sell or buy.

Second, history tends to repeat itself. You can use psychology to project the behavior of the market, as people tend to react in a similar manner if the same stimuli are present. For example, Bitcoin's price has regularly reacted in a bullish way to major news supporting the trend or businesses embracing cryptocurrencies.

Third, the market has the tendency to discount everything. Take note that all past, present, and future data are already factored in the present price of an asset. In the case of Bitcoin, it involves past, present, and future demand alongside present regulations covering digital currencies. The current price could reflect all present data that also involves the expectation and level of knowledge of Bitcoin traders. Therefore, you may choose to assess what the price is saying about the mood of the market to make sure that you are making wise estimates about price movements.

Fourth, what is more important compared to the why. Technicians are focusing more on the history of the price compared to specific factors, which have caused the price movement. Even though any number of factors could result in the price movement of a security in a certain manner, technicians normally take a more direct approach through the assessment of the present supply and demand.

Assessment of Trends

Assessment of the trends or the overall movement of digital currencies could help Bitcoin traders and investors. However, it can be difficult to single out these trends. Cryptocurrencies are normally volatile, and assessing a chart of the price fluctuations of Bitcoin may reveal a series of upward and downward trends.

However, you can study the volatility of the Bitcoin price through technical analysis. You can also determine the uptrend if you spot on a sequence of extreme downward or upward trends. In contrast, you could also single out a falling trend, when you are pinpointing a sequence of highs and lows. In addition, you may also need to consider sideway trends, in which the Bitcoin may follow a bit of upward or downward trend.

You must also remember that the trends normally come in various lengths such as short-term, mid-term, and long-term.

Spotting Moving Averages in Bitcoin

Another strategy that you can use to easily look for trends is to spot the moving averages, which could help in levelling the price fluctuations of a digital currency.

The simple moving average is the most basic form of moving averages. It is determined by calculating the average price of a unit over a specific period of time. For example, you could look at the price of Bitcoin over 30 days or 60 days.

Exponential moving average is another tool that you could use. This will provide you a better understanding of the current price values if you are crunching on the average. If you try to evaluate moving averages, you could gain a better understanding of when the price momentum may change. For example, when a 5-day moving average is falling below the moving average of the past 20 days, this change could signify a bullish market that is gradually becoming bearish.

The opposite is true if the trend is going against this direction and the shorter average rises above the longer average.

The Role of Bitcoin Volume in Technical Analysis

Take note that volume has a critical role in evaluating the Bitcoin price trends. High volume signifies strong price trends, while low volume indicates weaker price trends. When the Bitcoin price experiences a major loss or gain, you should ensure that you take a look at the volume.

For example, when the Bitcoin price is experiencing a long uptrend, and then abruptly declines in a day, you should check out the volume so you can gain a better understanding if this movement could signify a new trend or just a short setback.

In general, the rising prices could coincide with the rising volume. When the Bitcoin price is experiencing an upward trend, but the upward price is taking place in the midst of weak volume, it could signify a trend that is already running out of steam and could just fade away.

Trading Signals

The good thing about modern trading, especially in Bitcoin, is that you may choose to hire the services of professionals or firms to do the trading for you. There are signal providers who are trained in using technical analysis to send you alerts if they believe it is time to sell or buy BTCs. But take note that you have to pay a certain subscription fee to gain access to the trading signals.

Margin Trading

Margin trading is a good way to expand your investment capital, so you can make profit from market fluctuations. You can do this by borrowing the funds you need so you can make the trade and using the BTCs you own as collateral. For example, you have $10,000 to buy BTCs. Instead of purchasing with this cash, you can loan $90,000 and purchase $100,000 worth of Bitcoins using a leverage of 1:10. When the price increases by only 1 percent, you could gain 10 percent. But this could be risk as any price decrease by 5 percent will result in your capital losing 50 percent.

Because margin trading is risky, there are automated systems that you can use, which will allow you to sell if the market fluctuations are quite extreme. This could put a cap on your losses below the initial capital that you have already shelled out. In our example scenario, when the price is falling at 9 percent, then you could easily lose 90 percent of the capital. If this persists, then you can lose all your investments, which include the money that you have borrowed. To prevent such substantial loss, you can set up a margin call that will instantly exit the market if there are indications of extreme fluctuations.

a) Electronically Traded Funds (ETFs)

Another way to become profitable in Bitcoin margin trading is by using Electronically Traded Funds or ETFs. These funds have similar Bitcoin price tracks. But the fund does not actually hold the coins. Basically, this is only ideal and more accessible for day traders, as all trades conclude at the end of the day. The primary benefit of using ETFs is the cheaper fees compared to using primary market exchanges. You can also take advantage of 1:10 leverage, while the leverages that are often available on the exchanges totally depend on what other traders are offering.

b) Bitcoin Futures

Futures refer to the agreement which provides the trader the ability to make a purchase at a certain price and at a specific date in the future. You can use this when you own a significant amount of BTCs as a hedge, so you will avoid losing a lot of value when the price goes down. Speculators are using the futures to make some profit by projecting if the Bitcoin price at a specific time will be lower or higher.

Selling Bitcoins Online

Selling BTCs online is probably the easiest way to trade your digital currencies. There are three basic ways to sell BTCs online: direct trade, via online exchange, and through P2P trading.

In direct trading, you use websites that are offering this form of trading structure such as Bittylicious, BitBargain in the UK, and LocalBitcoins and Coinbase in the US. You first have to register as a seller, a process which verifies your identity. After the registration process, you can post a trade offer. The website will send you a notification if a buyer is interested in buying your BTCs. From here, your interaction is directly with the buyer, but you must use the website facilities to fulfill the trade.

Another way to sell your Bitcoins is to use exchange platforms. You have to confirm your identity, but in this situation, there is no need to do as much work in arranging the sale. The exchanges serve as an intermediary who is holding the BTCs of its members. In using the service, you will need to place a sell order, which includes the volume, the type of cryptocurrency you want to sell, as well as the price per unit. Once a member places a buy order that matches your sell order, the exchange will process the sale, and the currency will be credited to your nominated bank account.

Chapter 8 Quiz

Please refer to Appendix H for the answers to this quiz

1. What should be the first part of your investment or trading plan?

    A) Putting all your savings into the market

    B) Coming up with a plan

    C) Diversifying your portfolio

    D) Cashing out as soon as profit is made

2. What is one of the simplest, most reliable ways to make money with Bitcoin?

    A) Becoming a small-scale Bitcoin exchanger

    B) Dumping all your reserve funds into Bitcoin, hoping for the best

    C) Buying during upswings and selling on downswings

    D) Selling during upswings and buying on downswings

3. What is fundamental analysis?

    A) Looking at big trades in the market and copying them

    B) Inspecting the public ledger for transactions that might be fraudulent

    C) A traditional tool used by investors and traders to speculate the value of a stock

    D) Analyzing one's fundamental beliefs about investing and trading

4. What is most important in evaluating Bitcoin demand?

    A) Figuring out which transactions are made by genuine traders who are receiving Bitcoins other parties

    B) The number of daily transactions in total

C) Looking at the median price of Bitcoin

D) It is impossible to evaluate Bitcoin's demand

5. What is a dead Bitcoin?

   A) A Bitcoin used in a fraudulent transaction

   B) A Bitcoin that been hacked or stolen

   C) A Bitcoin that is in process from the buyer to the seller

   D) A Bitcoin which can no longer be accessed

6. Why is evaluating the supply of Bitcoin easy?

   A) Bitcoins are produced at a steady rate

   B) Bitcoins never change in value

   C) There is a cap on the number of Bitcoins in circulation

   D) The number of bitcoins in circulation never changes

7. True / False: Monitoring the news is a great way to dictate Bitcoin trades and investments.

8. What is capitalizing on correction?

   A) When a Bitcoin buyer makes a mistake, and sellers capitalize on it

   B) When a market has a surge or downfall, and traders make the most of an overreaction

   C) When investors hold their money too long, cash out at a loss, and buyers scoop up cheap Bitcoins

   D) When traders dump Bitcoins into the market to reduce the price, then buy them back as the price declines.

9. What is swing trading?

    A) A method used to figure out the turning points in short-term trends
    B) Trading large sums of Bitcoins at random
    C) Putting a small amount of money in the market to test its viability
    D) Creating hype for the market, then selling as the price increases.

10. Technical analysis looks for _____ and _____ to predict the market.

    A) CEOs, financiers
    B) News, hype
    C) Patterns, trends
    D) Buyers, sellers

11. What is a trading signal?

    A) A signal that tells you if it's time to buy or sell bitcoins
    B) An outbound signal sent on each trade
    C) An incoming signal received on each trade
    D) A signal sent when a trade is approved

12. What are ETFs?

    A) Euro Trading Funds
    B) Exchangeable Transfer Funds
    C) Electronically Traded Funds
    D) Electronically Transferred Finances

13. What is NOT a way to sell BTCs online?

A) Direct trade
B) Online exchange
C) P2P trading
D) Physical meetup

Bitcoin

Facts and Myths

Chapter 9

Bitcoin Facts and Myths

For the majority of the global population, the blockchain technology, cryptocurrencies and Bitcoin itself are topics that are shrouded in mystery. Because of its complexity and the need to have at least a working computer skill, it is not surprising that there are many myths, misconceptions, and misrepresentations about Bitcoin. In this Chapter, you will learn Bitcoin facts and myths that are crucial to understand if you wish to explore more about this digital currency.

Below are 20 facts about Bitcoins that you must know.

1. No central authority is controlling this cryptocurrency

Bitcoin is running on an open-source code. Therefore, anyone (regardless of if they are part of the network) can access the public ledger. No single government or private company is backing the generation of Bitcoins. Even Satoshi Nakamoto (the anonymous creator of Bitcoin) does not own the whole platform.

2. No one Has Seen Satoshi Nakamoto

The creator of Bitcoin, Satoshi Nakamoto, is anonymous. In fact, this name is believed to be his pseudonym. Despite the popularity of his creation, he has not appeared in public and no one has talked to him even over the phone. He only communicates in online forums. Nakamoto claims he is from Japan and was born in 1975.

Many experts don't believe this claim as the white paper he published in 2008 was written in perfect English, and his spellings are sometimes of British style. In addition, no documents or labels related to Japan were discovered in the software he was using. It is speculated that Nakamoto started developing the Bitcoin software as early as 2006 and invited other talented developers to his team. Later on, he formed a group and used the Japanese name as a code.

3. Bitcoin was used to buy two large pizzas for 10,000 BTCs, now worth around $26 million

In the initial years of Bitcoin, the early adopters were not so mindful of their Bitcoin accounts. In fact, Gavin Andresen freely gave away 10,000 BTCs, which was only around $50 in those days. Meanwhile, Laszlo Hanyez, an American programmer, holds the title as the first person to complete a real-world Bitcoin transaction. He ordered two large pizzas for 10,000 BTCs. He sent the Bitcoins to another early adopter in the UK who then ordered the pizza using his credit card. Even though it was only around $40 at that time, 10,000 BTCs are now more than $26 million.

4. The total Bitcoin computing capacity around the world is 256x faster compared to the computing speed of 500 supercomputers

As you have learned in this book, the production of Bitcoin relies on the miners who are using computer processing to solve complex mathematical problems to verify transactions. Because of the tight competition for earning Bitcoins, faster hardware is also being developed to keep up with the demand. This requires a significant amount of computing power to add more blocks in the system. As a result, Bitcoin companies have been built around the globe using a wide array of computers designed for mining Bitcoins.

Currently, Bitcoin mining has around 64 exaFLOPS (Floating Point Operations per second), which is used to gauge the processing speed in computing actual numbers. As a comparison, the top supercomputers in the world only have 0.250exaFLOPS, which means that the whole Bitcoin network is 256x faster compared to the best supercomputers in the world.

5. The number of Bitcoins will never exceed 21 million

Remember, Bitcoins are produced if a user confirms an added block in the chain. The rate of creating new blocks is flexible to make certain that only 6 blocks will be generated per hour or 2,016 blocks every 14 days. And for every 210,000 blocks, or every four years, the number of BTCs for every block will be slashed down to 50%.

This indicates a limit of 21 million BTCs, and it is estimated that the last Bitcoin will be produced sometime in early 2140. But take note that this estimate is based on present-day technology, and it can be difficult to project how the mining process will evolve with prospects of advanced technology in the future.

6. The attack on Mt. Gox is considered as the biggest thievery of all time

Mt. Gox was a cryptocurrency exchange that used to handle around 60% of Bitcoin transactions around the world. When its servers were attacked, its coffers contained around 800,000 BTCs, which is worth $450 million. The attack was regarded as the biggest thievery of all time, and because Bitcoin transactions cannot be reversed, the company only managed to recover around 190,000 BTCs.

7. A company sent a Bitcoin transaction into the outer space

Recently, a Bitcoin transaction was sent into outer space by Genesis Mining, a global company that specializes in selling digital currency mining contracts. The company sent a 3D model of a Bitcoin with an attached paper wallet via a weather balloon. The "package" was able to pass the Armstrong point and managed to travel a distance of 34 kms.

8. If you had purchased $100 worth of Bitcoins in 2009, you would be a multi-millionaire by now

Bitcoin's value exponentially increased since its creation in 2009. At present, 1 BTC is equivalent to $4,200.99. If you had purchased $100 worth Bitcoins in 2009, you would have around $140.033 million as of September 2017. One example of this is the case of Kristoffer Kock, who purchased 5000 Bitcoins in 2009 for about $30 when he was writing a thesis about encryption. He forgot about this purchase until Bitcoin became very popular in 2013. Upon checking his Bitcoin wallet, he was surprised that his 5,000 BTCs ballooned to around $886,000 or 5 million kroner at that time. This is now equivalent to around $21 million.

9. Bitcoin transactions use a significant amount of energy

As mining Bitcoin becomes more complicated over time, more and more processing power is required for mining. The average power consumption for every transaction, regardless of its size, is around 94 kilowatt hours, which is enough to power around three medium-sized homes in the US. In another perspective, the power requirement of Bitcoin today is also enough to completely charge a Tesla electric car.

10. Bitcoin's blockchain technology solves the problem of double spending

Bitcoin's blockchain is a public database, which does not need one authority. It is also operated by connected nodes that run the Bitcoin software. These nodes could validate the transactions and are capable of adding them to the ledger. At least every 10 minutes, a newly generated group of verified transactions will be added to the blockchain. This update is then disseminated to other nodes, which allows every network to keep its copy of the public ledger. This mechanism makes certain that the whole blockchain is aware if a certain amount is spent, which prevents double spending.

11. The biggest transaction in Bitcoin involved 194,993 BTCs recorded in 2013

In November 22, 2013, the largest Bitcoin transaction was recorded in the history of Bitcoin, which involved 194,993 BTCs, which was around 1.6% of all BTCs in circulation at that time. Some people believe this transaction involved Nakamoto himself, while others believe it was Richard Branson, who at that time announced his company Virgin Galactic would accept BTCs as payment.

12. The FBI owns one of the largest Bitcoin wallets in the world

Aside from Nakamoto, the Federal Bureau of Investigation (FBI) of the United States Government owns the largest Bitcoin wallet in the world. This was opened by the agency in 2013, when it shut down the operations of Silk Road and seized all BTCs from its coffers. The FBI acquired about 174,000 BTCs from Silk Road, and another 100,000 from the seizure of another underground market known as the Sheep Marketplace.

13. You can send BTCs with minimal or zero fees

The primary reason that banks are charging for transaction fees is greed. It costs them nothing to transfer money. This is just one of the numerous reasons why Bitcoin is becoming very popular among people who think they are being robbed by banking institutions for charging money for such an easy service. In using Bitcoins, you don't need to pay someone any fee, because no one owns the whole network. The fees are very minimal and they are voluntary.

14. Once you lose your wallet, you have lost your BTCs forever

The highest risk of owning BTCs is that you cannot recover them unless the other party returns your payment. That is why you should always make sure that your Bitcoin wallets are secured and you only deal with vendors that are trusted. In addition, when you lose your Bitcoin wallet without any backup, there is no way to recover them all. Be careful in spending as well as storing your BTCs.

15. Bitcoin was first used in the Dark Web

Bitcoin became a major currency used by members of the underground markets such as Silk Road, which was a concealed channel for online buyers for ordering drugs. In fact, the use of BTCs was the key for Silk Road's success. Aside from illegal drugs, Silk Road also offered other items such as hacking software, compromised credit card numbers, and fake IDs.

16. Bitcoin ignited the development of a new industry

The popularity of Bitcoin, ignited by its gradual acceptance from the mainstream public as well as several governments in the world, has contributed to the emergence of a new industry as well as related industries to Bitcoin. Experts estimate that today, Bitcoin is a $3 Trillion industry from the Bitcoin itself to Bitcoin mining companies and businesses such as cloud hosting and exchanges.

17. King's College is the First School in the World to Accept Bitcoins

King's College, located in New York, is an academic institution that is known for being a progressive entity. Because of this core value, it became the first school around the world to accept Bitcoins for paying tuition fees.

18. Minted Bitcoins were halted by the US Government

Bitcoin is a purely digital asset. But in 2013, one company called Casascius attempted to create physical BTCs. However, because it violated minting laws in the US, it was immediately shut down by the US Treasury.

19. Many BTCs are not in circulation

As a currency, BTCs should be used for buying products or services. However, because of its volatility and sudden rise, some BTC owners are not using them. Instead, they are just accumulating the currency in the hopes of gaining more value from its appreciation in the future. Some also noted that Satoshi Nakamoto has around 1 million BTCs and these are not circulated.

20. There Is a Bitcoin Boulevard in Netherlands

In Hague, Netherlands, there is a shopping district where most businesses are accepting Bitcoin payments. From coffee shops to boutiques, to movie houses to bars, you can enjoy them all and pay in BTCs.

20 Myths about Bitcoin

Now that we have learned some facts about Bitcoins, it is now time to debunk some myths and misconceptions surrounding this cryptocurrency.

Myth No. 1 - Bitcoin Is Completely Anonymous

Even though Bitcoin has been used in concealed transactions (mostly illegal dealings in the dark web) during its early days, it is not completely anonymous. The correct term to use in describing BTC transactions is pseudonymous, or partially anonymous. For every user in the network, there is an identifiable address (and, in some cases, several addresses). However, no one really knows who is behind these addresses. In BTC transactions, you should take note that each transaction is recorded on a totally accessible record that anyone can explore. Recently, several companies have been established and they have developed technologies to reveal the identity of some users in the Bitcoin network.

Myth No. 2 - Bitcoin is dying

The impending death of Bitcoin is one of the most common myths circulating online. Since its creation in 2009, many non-believers insist that Bitcoin will soon fade away, because it is part of a grand scam. The truth is, Bitcoin is presently at the golden age in its history, if we refer to the number of transactions in the blockchain every day. The main concern now is how to achieve scalability, because there is a need for the block size to be expanded so the network can handle more transactions.

Myth No. 3 - Bitcoin is used for tax evasion

There is a popular argument floating around about Bitcoin dealings: that these transactions are used to evade government mandated taxes. Rest assured that these rumors are false. Even though cash transactions in the Bitcoin network are pseudonymous, they are still subjected to tax once spent in the actual world.

Myth No. 4 - Bitcoin offers total transparency

It is not true that Bitcoin runs on absolute transparency. The personal details of the organizations and individuals behind particular addresses used in Bitcoin are often unknown. Furthermore, there are now existing privacy-specialist companies that will allow you to improve your privacy while using Bitcoin. Instead of being totally transparent or anonymous, Bitcoin is better described as being in the middle ground.

Myth No. 5 - Bitcoins are free

People ignorant of the mining process believe that Bitcoins are free because they come from nowhere. This is not true. Bitcoins are generated through a mining process, which requires extensive computing power. This process verifies the transactions by solving a sequence of mathematical problems. Miners who are able to verify the transaction and add a new block are rewarded with fresh BTCs on top of the fees that they may be given from the parties behind the transaction. Take note that in order to make money, you have to spend money, and at present, Bitcoin mining costs can exceed millions of dollars.

Myth No. 6 - Terrorists are using BTCs

Bitcoins break into television shows and movies with a poor image, as they are often depicted as the currency of terrorists or cyber criminals. The reality is, there is no actual evidence linking any terrorist group using Bitcoins in a massive scale. While BTCs are sometimes used for illegal dealings online, the security issues associated with the public ledgers used by Bitcoins make it a dangerous choice for terrorists as no matter how concealed the platform is, the transactions can still be traced. Cash is the safest form of payment.

Myth No. 7 - Bitcoin POS is impossible

Using a Point of Sale (POS) system for accepting BTC payments is currently impossible because of the time it will take to confirm the transactions and to ensure that double spending will not occur. However, BTC-enabled POS systems are now coming into existence. These include BitPremier, which sells luxury items such as high-end jewelry, sports car, and yachts. Since the transaction deals with luxurious items, customers are willing to wait for several hours, instead of taking the extra effort of paying in cash or in credit. Coffee shops and donut houses that are using POS for accepting BTCs are still not that widespread, but they are highly possible in the remote future.

Myth No. 8 - Bitcoins are worthless because the currency is not backed by any government or banks

Bitcoin naysayers who are not fully aware of the value of a decentralized payment system believe that Bitcoins are basically worthless because these are not supported by any government or banking system. There is an ongoing debate about this, which includes people who believe that the scarcity of BTCs is the primary trait that provides it value. On the other end of the spectrum, there are also people who claim that BTCs are valuable because they are needed to use the most popular and most secure public ledger in the world. Moreover, the value of a currency is not based on the backing of a government or a bank but by the consensus of people who agree that something has value. For example, USD is value because billions of people around the world agree that it has value.

Myth No. 9 - Quantum computers could break the security of Bitcoin

It is possible that quantum computers could break the security protocol of Bitcoin as well as the present-day banking systems that are depending on cryptography. However, this is considered to be a myth because quantum computers are yet to be developed.

Myth No. 10 - The high volatility of Bitcoin will make it worthless

Even though BTC has really high volatility based on its history and present movement, the trend is following the path of stability ever since the first BTCs were created in 2009. Most people who own BTCs in their wallets are not using them for their transactions, but rather keep them as a storage of value. And today, there are also different systems in using BTCs as payments that will allow you to avoid the high volatility linked with this digital currency. For instance, the company Coinbase will let you store value in USD or other conventional currencies before you make BTC transactions.

Myth No. 11 - Bitcoin is a Ponzi Scheme

Bitcoin cannot be considered as a Ponzi scheme because Satoshi Nakamoto, its founder, did not convince early investors that they will make substantial profit. Remember, Bitcoin is not controlled by a single point of power, because it is a decentralized system. Therefore, no promises of income are made by the platform. In addition, a Ponzi scheme typically mandates new investors to pay the earlier investors. This doesn't happen in Bitcoin, because the platform can work with any user, and it becomes more stable if more people are using it.

Myth No. 12 - New blocks cannot be generated when the 21 million cap is reached

It is true that after mining all the 21 million BTCs, no one can generate new coins. However, the network still requires upkeep and security. While the conventional rewards for mining will be eliminated, the creation of new blocks and confirmation of transactions are still crucial in the network. Those who are into mining today can still make revenue from charging transaction fees.

Myth No. 13 - Mining Bitcoin is just a waste of electricity

Is mining Bitcoins just a waste of electricity? This depends on your viewpoint. The fact is, using computing power has a purpose when it comes to BTC mining. This is to secure all the transactions in the public ledger. If you think this is not valuable, then it is really a waste of resources. If you think securing USD in banks is not valuable, then keeping the lights on is another waste of energy. While mining Bitcoins require a lot of computing power, this is an essential measure to prove that people are using their resources to earn BTC rewards.

Myth No. 14 - The Bitcoin network is already compromised

The myth about the Bitcoin network being hacked for some time now is one of the most common myths circulating online. Attacks on Bitcoin have only occurred to the servers of websites using BTC. It is the insufficient security of these third-party exchanges and wallets, not the Bitcoin platform itself, that lead to lost coins. There have been zero attacks against the Bitcoin blockchain itself that have resulted in lost BTCs.

Myth No. 15 - Bitcoin's CEO is now in jail

When people are reading about Bitcoins, they often find connections to Mt. Gox and Silk Road. Some people even think that the FBI seized the operations of Bitcoin in 2013, which is not true because it was Silk Road — the underground market for illegal drugs that was raided by FBI. When Mt. Gox collapsed in 2014, people thought it was the actual Bitcoin platform that was affected. Because not all people are able to easily identify the difference between Bitcoin and the companies who are trying to capitalize on its success, many people believed that Bitcoin's CEO is now in jail. But the reality is, personalities who have been arrested include: Charlie Shrem, the CEO of BitInstant; Mark Karpeles, the CEO of Mt. Gox; and Ross Ulbricht, the founder of Silk Road. Take note that these people are not associated with Bitcoin and the blockchain technology.

Myth N0 16 - Bitcoin is a fake currency

Bitcoin deniers often say that Bitcoin is a fake currency, citing reasons such as lack of government interference, lack of single authority, pure digital existence, and fluctuating value. However, it is not surprising that in our current system of fiat currencies, the volatility of a currency as well as the lack of government backing can make people nervous about BTCs.

Remember that a currency should be something of value that is divisible and scarce. This is something that Bitcoin can easily do, and in fact it performs better compared to USD and gold.

Myth No. 17 - Bitcoins will soon be replaced by Altcoins

The popularity of Bitcoin has resulted in the emergence of alternative coins or Altcoins, which great vary according to the groups they are trying to serve or the innovation involved. Some altcoins are generally improved version of Bitcoins, and there are many of them. Many people are worried that these altcoins will soon replace Bitcoins. But this is unlikely to happen because Bitcoin has a unique platform that is unprecedented and not yet replicated. Moreover, many altcoins are quite small and are used by smaller groups that make them less secure compared to BTC.

Myth No. 18 - Bitcoin is popular only in the West

Bitcoin started in the West, so it is natural that the early adopter will come from the region. In addition, the West also has some advantages when it comes to technological adaptation especially with cryptocurrencies. And most materials about Bitcoin are written in English, which make it more accessible to people who know the language. But despite of these hurdles, many Bitcoin hubs are now established in Asia and South America. Countries adopting the hubs include: Japan, Argentina, Singapore, the Philippines, and Brazil. Bitcoin communities and businesses are also emerging in the Middle East and Africa.

Myth No. 19 - The blockchain technology is more valuable and BTCs are not necessary

The open record and the high security of the blockchain is what provides Bitcoin its appeal. Hence, when people learn about this, they easily dismiss the importance of Bitcoin as a mere product of the Blockchain. But the reality is, mining is the power source of the Bitcoin platform, and without miners the blockchain will not operate.

Meanwhile, miners are doing the work for the reward they can gain, or else they will not spend time, money, and effort to mine for BTCs. As its natural incentive, BTC is essential to the operations of the Blockchain.

Myth No. 20 - Bitcoin has no advantage over credit cards or cash

When people learn that BTC can be used to purchase actual things in the real world, they may not be able to see what the cryptocurrency can offer over current payment methods such as credit cards and cash. Fortunately, it is quite easy to debunk this myth. There are several advantages in using BTCs over credit cards or cash. This includes the low transaction fees, which will save both parties as much as 3% when using credit cards. And in transferring money from one country to another, BTC has an obvious advantage because of the large remittance charges.

Bitcoin

Frequently Asked Questions

Chapter 10

Bitcoin FAQs

In this Chapter, we will go over the top 20 Frequently Asked Questions (FAQs) about Bitcoin.

1. Who regulates the Bitcoin protocol?

There is no single owner of the Bitcoin protocol, much like the fact that no single individual or organization owns the technology that enables us to send emails. Basically, Bitcoin is under the consensus control of Bitcoin users around the globe. And even if programmers are working on improving the open-source code, they cannot easily implement a change, because the users have the freedom to use the software as well as the version they want to use. The Bitcoin protocol can only work properly if all members are in consensus. Hence, the developers and users are protecting this consensus to keep the system running.

2. Can someone buy all existing BTCs?

It is important to remember that only a fraction of the BTCs are in circulation and available on the Bitcoin exchanges that are on sale. The competition in the Bitcoin market is very high, which means that the price of BTCs can easily rise or fall according to the law of demand and supply. In addition, new BTCs will still be produced for many decades to come. Even if there is someone who has all the wealth to purchase all BTCs available, it is impossible to just purchase all of them.

3. Are actual people really using BTCs today?

The number of individuals and businesses who are now using and accepting BTCs as payments is growing. This now includes brick-and-mortar stores such as coffee shops, restaurants, online stores, and even service-oriented organizations. Its acceptance is rapidly expanding despite of the fact that Bitcoin is still a very young technology.

4. Can users connive with each other to go against the Bitcoin protocol?

Again, it is not easy to change the Bitcoin protocol. Any user in the network who is not following the rules will not be able to use the system properly. In its current version, it is not possible for the network to allow double spending without a confirmed signature. Therefore, it is almost impossible to produce unregulated amounts of BTCs from nowhere, disrupt the network, spend other BTC funds, or the like.

5. How can you acquire BTCs?

You can acquire BTCs when you are selling goods or services and you are paid in Bitcoins. You can also buy the currency at reliable Bitcoin exchanges or earn the currency as a reward for mining in the protocol. While it is also possible to look for people who want to sell their BTCs in exchange for PayPal or credit card payment, a majority of the current BTC exchanges do not allow this method. This is because of the possibility of purchasing Bitcoins in PayPal and then reversing the transaction, which is known as a chargeback.

6. Is there a limit to the number of Bitcoins that can be created?

The current Bitcoin protocol limits the number of Bitcoins that can be created to 21 million BTCs. But this is not actually a limit because the transactions can still be in a smaller denomination. Take note that there are around 1 million bits in 1 BTC, and the currency is divisible by 8 decimal places. The currency can be broken down into smaller units if required in the future.

7. Is it easy to make a payment in BTC?

BTC payments are easier to make compared to a credit card or debit card payments. You can even receive payments without a merchant account. The payments are made via wallet application, either on a smartphone or a computer using the address of the recipient. Many BTC wallets today are also using QR codes to store the address of the recipient.

8. Is Bitcoin unfairly beneficial to early advocates?

It is true that early advocates of BTCs have managed to accumulate a substantial number of BTCs, because they have invested their own time and resources in investing in a technology that was not guaranteed to become successful. Most of the early advocates in fact were not mindful of their expenditures of their BTCs prior to the popularity of the digital currency. This is quite similar to investing in a startup business that may either go bankrupt or become profitably successful.

9. Is the Bitcoin protocol trustworthy?

The trust in Bitcoin is mainly sourced from the fact that it requires zero trust at all. The protocol is decentralized and completely open source, which means anyone can access the whole source code anytime. All the Bitcoin produced and all the transactions that happened can be easily consulted in real time.

10. Is Bitcoin another bubble?

The price of Bitcoin has risen quite fast in the recent years. However, this does not mean that it is another bubble or an artificial valuation that will surely result in a fall because of market correction. The cause of the fluctuation of the Bitcoin price is based on the choices of individuals in the market.

11. Can you make a profit in Bitcoin?

Bitcoin is a developing innovation and the business opportunities that are associated with this development also involve risks. Take note that there is no assurance that Bitcoin will continue to rise in value. You need to develop the right mindset and understand the whole mechanism to be profitable with Bitcoin.

12. Is Bitcoin completely digital?

Like credit cards and online banking systems, Bitcoins is completely digital. You can use it to pay for your online purchases. Your balances will be stored in a public network, which cannot be easily changed by anyone. To put it simply, members of the Bitcoin protocol have the exclusive rights to control their funds, and they cannot be easily lost just because they are digital.

13. What will happen if you lose your Bitcoins?

If you lose your wallet, your money will be out of circulation. In the case of lost Bitcoins, they are still in the block chain similar to other BTCs, but they will remain idle forever, unless you can still find your private keys that will allow you to access the funds.

14. Is there a possibility that Bitcoins will be devalued in the future?

Yes. History is filled with fiat currencies that have dramatically failed and became obsolete such as the Zimbabwean dollar and the German Papiermark. Even though these currency devaluations were normally caused by too much inflation, which does not affect Bitcoins, there is always the possibility that this cryptocurrency will become obsolete because of political issues, rising competition, and technical flaws.

15. Is there a chance that Bitcoin will become a mainstream currency?

Even though Bitcoins are gradually becoming more accepted by individuals, businesses, and governments around the world, the whole protocol is not yet ready to become a full-scale payment network similar to fiat currencies, PayPal, or credit cards. However, the prospect is good that the Bitcoin protocol and the cryptocurrency will become a major currency in the near future.

16. Are Bitcoin users protected in using the Bitcoin protocol?

The Bitcoin protocol allows people to transact with each other using their own terms. Every user can receive and send BTC payments like a cash payment, but they can also participate in a more sophisticated agreement. Multiple signatures can allow a transaction to be accepted by the consensus of the network only if a specific number of persons agree to verify the transaction. This opens the gate to develop arbitration services in the future to allow independent parties to reject or approve a deal if the parties cannot come into agreement.

17. Is Bitcoin legal?

At present, no government has declared Bitcoin as an illegal currency. But there are some jurisdictions such as China, Russia, and Argentina that prohibits the use of foreign currencies in their jurisdictions, which includes Bitcoins. Other territories such as Thailand also limit the licensing of Bitcoin-related organizations like Bitcoin exchanges and wallets.

18. Can you accrue tax liability when you use Bitcoins?

Remember, Bitcoin is not considered a fiat currency and it has no legal tender status like the USD and other major currencies around the world. However, tax liability can still be accrued when you use it for payments. There is now a wide range of legislation in various jurisdictions that could cause capital gains, income, sales, and other forms of taxation that will arise with BTC.

19. Can Bitcoin be regulated?

The Bitcoin network cannot be changed without the consensus of its members. Trying to add a special rights or privilege to a single authority in the process of the protocol is quite impossible. Any organization who has the resources may, however, invest in Bitcoin mining to control a majority computational capacity of the network. But there is no assurance that they can maintain this power because it will require a significant amount of money and there is tight competition among the largest Bitcoin miners in the world.

20. Is Bitcoin used by cyber criminals?

Bitcoin is now considered as a currency, and any currency can be used for both legal and illegal purposes. The current banking system, credit card networks, and cash largely surpass Bitcoin when it comes to its usage in financial crimes. In fact, Bitcoin can substantially innovate the payments systems. The advantages of this innovation are usually regarded to be far more beneficial than their possible downsides.

The End

Thank you very much for taking the time to read this book. We sincerely hope you have gained something of value. We are here to serve you and every encouragement from you means a lot to us.

If you enjoyed this book, please be kind enough to review us (by clicking on the green button below) and let us know what you liked about it or what you would love to see. This will help us produce better content for you folks and also help buyers out there make an informed decision when looking to make a purchase. Thank you so much for taking the time to leave a review!

Please Review

Follow me

To receive notifications from Amazon whenever I release a new book feel free to follow me by clicking the orange follow button on my author page. Clicking on the below picture will take you directly to my author page on Amazon where you will find the button. You can also reach me via email: JamesTudor@yahoo.com or www.MillenniumPublishingLimited.com

Appendix A

Please find below the solution to the quiz presented in chapter 1

Question Number	Answer
1	D
2	B
3	D
4	A
5	C
6	A
7	D
8	B
9	C
10	A

Appendix B

Please find below the solution to the quiz presented in chapter 2

Question Number	Answer
1	A
2	C
3	B
4	D
5	A
6	B
7	False
8	A
9	D

Question 7 – False: It is irrelevant to compare the two because Bitcoin will not replace the US Dollar as the reserve currency of the world.

Appendix C

Please find below the solution to the quiz presented in chapter 3

Question Number	Answer
1	D
2	A
3	D
4	C
5	B
6	A
7	C
8	D
9	False

Question 9 - False: The core structure of blockchain means that, currently, transactions take longer than centralized options.

Appendix D

Please find below the solution to the quiz presented in chapter 4

Question Number	Answer
1	C
2	A
3	B
4	C
5	A
6	C
7	D
8	True
9	A

Question 8 – True: Power and hardware costs typically outweigh any profits a freelancer would make.

Appendix E

Please find below the solution to the quiz presented in chapter 5

Question Number	Answer
1	B
2	False
3	A
4	C
5	D
6	B
7	C
8	A
9	D
10	B

Question 2 – False: Bitcoins are not controlled centrally, so keep track of them!

Appendix F

Please find below the solution to the quiz presented in chapter 6

Question Number	Answer
1	C
2	D
3	A
4	A
5	C
6	B
7	True
8	A

Question 7 – True: Many currencies in the past have been devalued.

Appendix G

Please find below the solution to the quiz presented in chapter 7

Question Number	Answer
1	D
2	A
3	D
4	D
5	C
6	C

Appendix H

Please find below the solution to the quiz presented in chapter 8

Question Number	Answer
1	B
2	A
3	C
4	A
5	D
6	C
7	False
8	B
9	A
10	C
11	A
12	C

| 13 | D |

Question 7 – False: It is impossible to always monitor the latest news, and the market adjusts too quickly to make informed decisions.

Made in the USA
Middletown, DE
28 December 2017